My Fun with Learning

5

Parents
as
Teachers

by Jenny Tesar

Illustrated by Frank Bolle

Cover Illustration by Jo Palseno

The Southwestern Company

Nashville, Tennessee

CONTENTS

About the Author

Jenny Tesar is a distinguished author, editor, and teacher whose primary concern is childhood education, especially in the areas of science and computer technology. For six years she taught at the junior high school level in the school systems of Monterey, California, and Long Island, New York, where she became expert in understanding children and their educational needs.

Her work as a writer is well known to readers of Grolier's *The New Book of Knowledge* and *The New Book of Popular Science,* for which she has written many articles. For seven years she has been a major contributor to the *Encyclopedia Americana* annuals. She is the author of the children's book *Introduction to Animals,* the first volume in the *Wonders of Wildlife* series, which she served as chief consultant. She was also editor of the *Illustrated Encyclopedia of the Animal Kingdom* series.

Jenny Tesar received her bachelor's degree in science from Cornell University in Ithaca, New York, and her master's degree in science education from Oregon State University in Corvallis, Oregon. Since completing her formal education, she has written more than 100 articles on general science, biology, computer science, and other educational topics, and has been the author of textbooks, filmstrips, teachers' guides, and educational computer software.

Chapter One

THE JOY OF LEARNING

YOUNG CHILDREN ARE IN LOVE with the world. Naturally curious and eager to explore, they want to touch, taste, see, and smell everything around them. They have dozens of questions and hope their parents have the answers. In fact, according to research at the University of Chicago reported by columnist Joan Beck in her book *How to Raise a Brighter Child:* "Your child has already developed half of his total adult intellectual capacity by the time he is four years old and 80 percent of it by age eight. After age eight, regardless of what kind of schooling and environment your child has, his mental abilities can only be altered by about 20 percent."

Numerous studies have shown that parental involvement is an important factor in developing children's potential and in determining how successful children will be—not only in school but throughout their lives. *The more involved the parents, the more successful their children will be.*

As you will discover in this book, you do not need a deep knowledge of teaching methods to help your children. There are many activities you can share with your children that will build learning skills. The goal is to prepare your children to get the greatest possible benefit from their formal education, and to convince them that learning is not limited to the classroom.

A World of Talent to Be Used

Not knowing how to read or reading with difficulty cripples the development of other skills. It puts people at a severe disadvantage in school and in society as a whole. Talented people may never realize their potential.

Until recently, it was assumed that anyone who had completed the fifth grade was literate. It was believed that the illiteracy rate in the United States was only half of 1 percent. But a report released by the U.S. Department of Education in 1986 presented a very different, and alarming, picture. It indicated that 17 to 21 million adults in the United States cannot read. Most of these people are under the age of 50, and many have attended high school. Even more disheartening is evidence that many additional millions of Americans are *functionally illiterate.* Although they have some reading ability, they cannot read simple instructions, address an envelope well enough to ensure postal delivery, write checks, or figure the correct change from a store purchase.

The consequences are staggering in terms of unhappiness, lost business productivity, and the cost of unemployment, crime, and social services.

If someone in your family has a literacy problem or if you would like to volunteer in the fight against illiteracy, write to The Coalition for Literacy, 50 East Huron Street, Chicago, IL 60611.

ABC'S OF HOME INSTRUCTION

There are many skills you can teach your children and much knowledge that you can share.

1. *Communication skills.* The ability to use language to gain and to share information. There are four communication skills: reading,

writing, speaking, and listening.

2. *Learning skills.* The ability to find information and the confidence to learn by oneself.

3. *Observation skills.* The ability to learn about the environment by using all the senses.

4. *Thinking skills.* The ability to look intelligently at a problem, think it through, and evaluate solutions.

5. *Creative skills.* The ability to use imagination.

The Value of Home Instruction

Making learning a priority has many benefits.

1. It develops positive attitudes toward learning and increases children's desire for knowledge.

2. It enriches children's worlds and broadens their horizons.

3. It builds educational skills needed to become happy, productive members of society.

4. It is emotionally satisfying and builds strong bonds between parents and children.

5. It enables parents to recognize their children's talents and limitations, and provides insights into children's problems and needs.

6. It makes parents better judges of the effectiveness of the education their children receive at school.

7. It gives children an understanding of the responsibilities they will have when they become parents.

Knowing how to read is a skill needed dozens of times each day. For instance, you carefully read instructions on a bottle before giving medicine to your child.

LITERACY: THE KEY TO SUCCESS

Most of what we learn is learned through language, through listening to others, or through reading what others have written. Language enables us to understand people and events that we cannot observe directly.

Until the 20th century, most knowledge was passed from one person to another through word of mouth. People were apprenticed to experts, who told them, for example, how to build a wall or treat a sick animal or prepare a legal case. Now, however, most knowledge is passed through books and other printed materials. As a result, it is essential to be able to read.

The ability to read and write is called *literacy*. The power of literacy cannot be overestimated. It enables people to comprehend and learn new subjects, to succeed in careers, and to be responsible members of the community and good citizens.

USING THIS BOOK

This book is designed to help your children develop their capacity for learning. Much of the emphasis is on development of reading skills. Other subjects are covered as well, for it is important to seek a balance in the experiences you provide for your children. While reading is important, it is not the only aspect of learning. Learning involves intellectual, creative, social, emotional, and physical skills.

You will find it helpful to read through this book to get an overview of the types of activities that will help strengthen your children's educational development. Then you will find it helpful to read certain chapters as needed. For instance, Chapter Four contains much information for the time when your children are eager to learn how to print letters. Chapter Eleven contains many suggestions on how to make trips meaningful experiences. These are just two examples of the usefulness of this book.

Every chapter includes activities that can be used to extend children's experiences and reinforce learning skills. It will be unlikely that your children will want to do all the suggested activities. Different children have different likes, dislikes, and needs, so some activities will be suitable for your children and others will not. You will help your children most if you use only those activities that interest them and that are appropriate for their abilities and level of maturity. It is better to save for a future time any activities that appear to be too difficult.

Chapter Two

ENRICHING YOUR CHILD'S ENVIRONMENT

CHILDREN WANT TO IMITATE their parents. This is a key to early learning. If children see you reading for pleasure or knowledge, they too will want to read. If they see you using dictionaries and encyclopedias to learn facts, they too will want to expand their knowledge. If they see you doing crossword puzzles and playing word games, they too will want to develop the vocabulary skills needed for these activities.

It never is too late to set a good example, but the earlier you begin, the more benefits your children will derive. It is worth repeating that research has shown that the most active period of intellectual growth occurs between birth and age four. By the time children are four years old, they have developed half their adult intellectual capacity; this figure jumps to 80 percent by age eight. In addition, many educators believe the training children receive from parents is the single most important factor in determining how successful children will be in school.

ATTITUDES ARE CRUCIAL

Parental attitudes toward children and their achievements are of great importance. Positive attitudes encourage children. Negative attitudes retard learning. Ignoring children and their accomplishments is also harmful.

Did you know that Albert Einstein took so long to learn to speak that his parents thought he was retarded? That Thomas Edison did so poorly during his first months of school that his teacher thought he was not bright?

Children differ greatly in the rate at which they learn. Some are ready to read and write when they are four or five, but most are not ready for these skills until they are six. Such differences are normal and not an indication of a child's intelligence. And they are not something for you or your children to worry about.

It is not helpful to try to speed your children's rate of learning by pushing them to do things they are not ready to do. Instead, it is better to choose activities they respond to and enjoy. For example, if children want to play over and over again with a six-piece puzzle, do not pressure them into trying a ten-piece one. They are strengthening skills every time they do that six-piece puzzle. In good time, they will reach for the more advanced puzzle.

You will often notice that learning seems to occur in spurts. This too is normal.

Parents are important role models. When they have positive attitudes toward books, their children also develop a love of books and an interest in reading.

10

CHOOSING BOOKS

There are many thousands of books written and illustrated especially for children. Each year there are thousands of new titles. These include all kinds of works: novels, fairy tales, poems, biographies, and nonfiction materials about animals, airplanes, religion, foreign lands, and other subjects.

Each book is appropriate for a certain range of ages. The appropriate range depends largely on sentence length, difficulty of vocabulary and concepts, and subject matter. No book can be recommended with certainty for any one child. A book that is right for one five year old may be too simple or too advanced for another.

Here are some general guidelines to follow when choosing books for your children:

1. Choose materials that are age-appropriate. Children will dislike reading if they find the material boring or too difficult to understand. Many books and types of books are appropriate over a wide

ENCOURAGEMENT IS THE KEY

Children who are encouraged keep trying, even if at first their efforts to master a skill are disappointing. To encourage your children to continue their efforts:

DO be optimistic about their abilities. Provide praise, affection, and understanding. Establish a warm atmosphere in your home. Make learning experiences meaningful but fun. Provide challenges appropriate for your children's ages and skill levels.

DO NOT be sarcastic or impatient. Do not make fun of failure. Do not make negative comparisons of one child with another. Do not pressure children to achieve. Do not make learning a regimented experience. Do not provide challenges you know the children are unable to meet.

range of ages. A good picture book can interest the same child year after year. A good story is timeless.

2. Choose a variety of materials: fiction, nonfiction, poetry, contemporary works, and children's classics.

3. Choose things the children can relate to. For instance, farm children do not want to read only about city life. Find books that portray the kind of life the children know. Otherwise, youngsters may come to believe that books have no relationship to their lives.

4. Choose attractive books. This is particularly important for prereaders and reluctant readers. Are there lots of illustrations? Can children relate to the illustrations? Older children appreciate good illustrations as well.

5. Choose books that meet your standards. Are the characters interesting? Is the book truthful? What is the book's message? What are the values shown in the story?

Learning About Books

Children's librarians are able to make suggestions on which books are most suitable for your children. Ask whether the library receives *The Booklist, The Horn Book Magazine,* or other periodicals that review children's books. Check the library's lists of recommended children's books. Examine books designed to help parents develop children's reading skills. These often include lists of books children admire. Other valuable sources of recommendations include teachers and other parents.

Books Borrowed and Bought

Many excellent books can be borrowed from public and school libraries. Make use of these resources. In addition, build a home library for your children. This need not be large, but it should contain a collection of nursery rhymes, an anthology of classic children's stories, some well-illustrated alphabet and counting books.

As children get older, add fairy tales, animal stories, and books related to the children's interests. Some of the books you purchase for your children can be inexpensive paperbacks or used books found at tag and garage sales. But at least a few of the books should be beautifully produced and filled with illustrations of high quality. Chances are these books will be treasured long after the toys of childhood have been thrown away.

It is good practice to involve your children in the purchase of books. This familiarizes them with bookstores and heightens their interest in the books they own. For instance, for a birthday you might give children money with which to buy books, and then go with them to purchase the present. Although the choice should be theirs, you can provide useful guidance. If they have difficulty in choosing between two wonderful books, you might return to the store later and buy the second book as a surprise gift.

Buy books for yourself, too. Choose books that will enrich your life and your children's lives as well. Songbooks, poetry, inspirational books, myths, and fables are among the books you and your children can enjoy together.

CHILD-CARE PROGRAMS

Enrolling children in nursery schools or other child-care programs is often a necessity when both parents work during the day. But even if both parents do not have to work, enrolling children in a preschool program can provide an opportunity for them to learn how people behave in groups and how to get along with both children and adults. It can help them develop independence and a sense of self-sufficiency, and it offers the possibility of playing with equipment not available at home.

In some communities, parents have only a limited choice of such programs. Elsewhere, a broad selection exists, ranging from baby-sitting services to nursery schools and day-care centers. Which program is best for your children depends in large part on the children's personalities, their individual needs, and their stages of development.

Child-care programs can provide challenges and enriching experiences that supplement activities provided by you in your home.

What to Look For

It is important to evaluate a child-care program before enrolling your children. Visit the program and speak with the administrators. Ask permission to sit in on classes and group activities. Try to answer these ten questions:

1. What are the program's goals and objectives?

2. What does the program consist of? Is there storytelling as well as play? How about music, crafts, art? Do the activities seem appropriate for the goals and objectives? Do they seem appropriate for your children? Do they add to, not just repeat, activities that you provide at home?

3. What are the qualifications of the members of the staff? Do they understand child development? Do they have good verbal skills? Make a point of having conversations with the people who work with your children.

4. What are the attitudes of the staff? Are they happy, outgoing, and excited about taking care of children? Do they treat children with affection? Do they know them well?

5. Are the facilities clean and attractive? Are there separate and safe areas for noisy play and quiet play? Is there sufficient space indoors and out?

6. Are there plenty of books, drawing materials, and toys? Are these where children can reach them? Is the furniture child-sized?

7. How large are the groups? The best programs emphasize small groups, so each child receives plenty of attention.

8. Do the children seem happy? Are they busy doing interesting things?

9. Is the program licensed by the state? Inquire as to whether it meets standards established by national or state organizations.

10. What are the costs?

How to Find Good Child Care

The best recommendations usually come from other parents. For this reason, it is important to talk with people who have children of the same age or slightly older than your children. Do the children of these parents seem to benefit from the programs?

Your family doctor or librarian may provide a directory of local child-care programs. You also may call the school superintendent's office to learn which programs the school recommends.

Chapter Three

BUILDING IMPORTANT
FOUNDATIONS

EVEN BEFORE BABIES BEGIN TO SPEAK, they listen to words used by adults and learn to identify objects. It is never too early for parents to lay the foundations for success in listening, speaking, reading, and other educational skills.

The most important thing you can develop in young children is self-confidence. You can lay the groundwork for this by putting them at ease through dealing with them in a relaxed, supportive manner. Each time you give them new activities, make sure they receive tasks at which they can easily succeed. What is important is not how quickly—or how much—your children learn, but that they acquire a thorough grasp of the material. Children enjoy success as much as adults do.

Young children like to do things over and over. They will return again and again to a puzzle they have already mastered, to a favorite toy or book, to a simple set of blocks. This is fine. Children learn by repetition. Each time they repeat an activity, they learn something new. Each time they play again with a toy, they use their imaginations to see it in a different way. This helps build the foundations and self-confidence for learning new concepts and exploring new things. So when children ask you to read them a particular story for what seems like the hundredth time, do not hesitate.

Even before they can talk, children let you know whether they are enjoying themselves. If they like the games and toys you choose, they will smile and actively participate. If they are bored or have had enough for the moment, they will get restless or cranky. Let them play on their own for a time or permit them a nap.

HOW TODDLERS LEARN

Before they develop language skills, young children learn in four main ways:

1. *Imitation.* Children see you open a book and turn its pages, so they do the same thing.

2. *Trial and error.* When children pile blocks all askew, the blocks tumble to the floor. But when the blocks are carefully centered one above another, children discover that the blocks will remain in place.

3. *Natural consequences.* When children touch a hot object, it hurts; thus they learn not to do it again.

4. *Logical consequences.* Some lessons are too dangerous to allow children to learn by one of the above methods. For example, you do not want your children to run into the road or play with kitchen

Simple puzzles help toddlers master important concepts about space and encourage small muscle development.

knives. As a result, you must tell the children clearly that such behavior can be harmful. If children insist on doing something you have indicated is forbidden, stop them and provide another activity. Thus, if children play outdoors and wander into the road, take them indoors. Let them know they will soon have another chance to play.

STIMULATE THE SENSES

Gathering and interpreting information about the environment involves all five senses. We learn the jingle of a telephone, the scent of roses, whether a book is right side up. We discriminate between the voice of Mommy and that of a stranger, the taste of an orange and a banana, the feel of velvet and wood.

Hearing

You can stimulate young children's sense of hearing by introducing them to a variety of sounds. Rattles, little bells tied to socks and shoes, wind chimes, and plastic squeak toys are among the sound-making objects that enchant babies. Later, they will enjoy experimenting with toy musical instruments. You will help your children by spending time singing and speaking to them. Do so while holding them in your arms and while standing at various distances from them. You also will help them by playing the radio and phonograph records for them, but take care not to set the sound level too high.

Sight

How can you stimulate seeing? By hanging bright objects across or over a baby's crib, by making puppets and stuffed animals appear, disappear, and reappear, by playing peek-a-boo, and by placing floating toys in baby's bath.

It is good to let babies play with ordinary household items, such as sponges and plastic spoons and cups. You also will help children if you show them their reflections in a mirror. Point to and say the names of various parts of the face. Point out the corresponding parts on your face.

Play ball together and show children how to blow bubbles. Let children stack blocks and move rings on and off a stick. Provide crayons and paper for scribbling. Show how different color crayons make different color scribbles. Name and talk about the colors in pictures you look at together.

Touch

You can stimulate feeling by massaging a baby as you change the baby's diapers. You also can help by giving young children furry stuffed animals and soft dolls. Objects of many different textures will stimulate feeling: terry cloth towels, silky scarves, feathers, sponges, plastic rings, rubber balls, cardboard, and wooden spoons.

Playing "let's pretend" with toys stimulates children's imaginations and gives them a chance to practice language skills.

Taste

When feeding children, identify the food. Show how to taste it. Ask whether they like the taste.

Smell

It is good practice to show young children that different objects have different scents. Let them smell flowers, foods, soaps, and perfumes. You may have to show young children how to smell. Try putting an object under your nose and showing the children how you sniff air.

18

ENCOURAGE LANGUAGE

Children begin to speak only after they have had many opportunities to hear adults speak. Communicate with babies and toddlers by talking and singing to them. Recite nursery rhymes and stories you know by heart. Point to things as you name them. Be attentive to their efforts to talk. Tell them Daddy or Mother is coming home. Tell them, "Daddy's home" or "Mother's home."

As you wash children's hands, use words such as *soap, water, towel, wet, dry, clean,* and *dirty.* As you dress them, talk about the articles of clothing, colors, snaps, and flowers on the fabric. As you prepare food, explain what you are doing: slicing apples, peeling potatoes, washing lettuce.

While you are playing with your children, use words to explain what is happening: "Here is a ball. We can roll the ball." As they become accustomed to hearing words and relating them to specific objects or actions, they will incorporate the words into their vocabularies.

Experts recommend that parents speak properly with children, that they use words and verb tenses correctly. Do not use your children's baby words or criticize their mistakes. If a child says "I swimmed today," you can say "Yes, I swam today too." Children will learn to correct themselves.

One of the best things you can do for toddlers is to show them how to pretend. This stimulates their imagination and gives them opportunities to try out language skills. Let them stir a wooden spoon in a pot while you are preparing a meal. Show them how to hold a doll and pretend it is a baby. Later, children will treat the doll as a friend, dressing it, feeding it, talking to it.

Small brooms, stuffed animals, toy telephones, doll houses, dump trucks, and fire engines are great for pretending. Blocks and boxes can be used to build houses, stores, barns, churches, and garages. Musical instruments can be created out of pots (drums), kitchen shakers (rattles), and cardboard paper towel rolls (horns).

BUILD THINKING SKILLS

An effective way to build thinking skills is to give children simple problems to solve. You might show them how nesting toys or measuring cups fit one inside the other. Place the items in front of the children and let them try to make a nest. They will gradually discover that small items can fit into large items, and that large ones will not fit into small ones.

Children need to learn concepts about space. Most activities that develop physical skills also develop a sense of space. For example, place a toy close to a baby for easy reach. Then move it a bit away, so the baby must reach farther to hold it. Put two blocks out of easy reach, one to either side, so the baby learns which arm to use to reach for things.

You also can show the meanings of directional words. When lifting a child up or putting the child down, say *up* and *down*. Wave the child's hands one at a time, saying *right hand, left hand*. Put the child's hands *in* water, then pull them *out*. You can do similar things with puppets and dolls.

DEVELOP PHYSICAL SKILLS

It is important to develop physical skills as well as mental skills. In fact, some physical skills must be mastered if children are to do well in school. Eye-hand coordination is needed for writing. So is the ability to hold a pencil correctly.

Many activities will develop both large muscles, such as those in the arms and legs, and small muscles, such as those in the fingers.

Large muscles are developed by crawling, walking, running, climbing, and playing ball, as well as by carrying objects and pulling and pushing toys.

When your children are ready, introduce them to the local playground. Show them how to walk on tiptoe, do somersaults, and stand on one foot. Play games such as Ring Around the Rosie and London Bridge Is Falling Down. Teach them how to ride tricycles.

Ask the children to perform practical tasks, too, such as putting clothes on hangers, sweeping the floor, and bringing you a book or other item. All these activities help them learn to coordinate their eyes and bodies.

Young children benefit from playing with modeling clay or other materials. Show them how to mold the material into different shapes. If you provide plastic pop beads, they will learn to put them together and pull them apart. Show them how to string beads. Begin with large beads and progress to smaller beads. Let them draw with crayons and use fingerpaints. Show them how to draw a straight line. Later, show how to make circles and squares.

Peg and hammer sets, blocks, jigsaw puzzles, small cars and trucks, toy telephones, wind-up toys—all are fun to play with, and all strengthen small muscle development. These muscles also are developed when children perform practical activities, such as using scissors, opening a door by turning the knob, and turning a water faucet on and off.

Chapter Four

GETTING READY TO READ

IN LEARNING TO READ, children have to go through many of the same steps an adult goes through in learning to read a foreign language, particularly a foreign language that uses an unfamiliar alphabet. The children have to learn what the printed marks represent, that those marks are arranged in groups called words, that the words are arranged in a specific way on a page, that various sounds are associated with the printed marks, and on and on and on. It is anything but easy. Learning to read takes practice. And patience and guidance on your part. But what a thrill it is for the children—and for you—when they show that they too can read a book.

The four language arts are listening, speaking, reading, and writing. It is important to extend and encourage all these skills. Many activities that focus on one skill also help develop others. For instance, when you ask your children to discuss something you read to them, you are building their listening skills and verbal skills. You also are laying the foundation for your children to understand the things they themselves will read.

Just as important as the skills themselves are your children's attitudes toward these skills. Be sure that activities are fun and are geared toward the children's present skill levels. It is good to challenge your children, but make certain that successes far outnumber failures. Your goal is to build positive, happy attitudes toward learning and reading.

LISTENING SKILLS

Practice in understanding and following directions will build listening skills. Thus, it is good to ask children to perform simple tasks: Please bring me the book that is on the table in my bedroom. Please fill a big glass with water and give it to your sister. Please put on your brown coat and brown hat. Please draw a green house with a red door and three windows.

When you play games that require children to listen, you are helping them learn to listen. Start a story, then ask the child to provide an ending. The child has to listen closely during the first part of the story in order to give an appropriate ending. The game of Simon Says requires close attention and reinforces directional skills, such as left-right and up-down.

If you imitate natural sounds and ask children to identify them, you will help the children's ability to listen. Ask your children to make sounds for you to identify. Go outdoors with them and make a list of all the sounds the children hear in ten minutes. Can they identify each of the sounds?

SPEAKING SKILLS

You will build your children's enthusiasm for communicating by providing opportunities for them to tell you about their activities. Frequent short conversations help more than an occasional half-hour talk. Let them speak at their own pace. Pay attention when they speak to you, setting a good example of how to listen. Do not divide your attention between them and the newspaper or TV—children may conclude that you are not interested in what they have to say. If they are eager to converse at a time that is inconvenient for you, explain that you must first finish what you are doing, but you want to hear their tale afterward.

Speak clearly so they can distinguish between sounds and understand what you are saying. If children have difficulty making a sound, help them practice the sound.

Rebus stories, which use pictures to represent words and syllables, help build reading comprehension and thinking skills.

Building Vocabulary

People have two vocabularies. Their listening and reading vocabulary is large. It consists of all the words they understand when listening or when they read words. Their speaking vocabulary is much smaller. It consists of the words they understand well enough to speak or write themselves.

When you introduce words to children who do not yet read, they will first incorporate the words into their listening vocabulary. It may take a while for them to use the words themselves. When you introduce a word, use it in a sentence. This gives children important clues to the meaning, just as seeing an unfamiliar word in a printed sentence makes it easier to figure out.

Introduce only one or two words at a time. Find occasions to use or review the words during the next few days. Children may forget words if they do not hear them often.

Among the words that should become part of children's speaking vocabularies are color words. Play a color sentence game in which the children must use the color word in a sentence. For example, you might say, "I see something red." The children cannot just point or say "car." They must respond, "The car is red." At first, play the game using only a few colors. Gradually add other colors and more challenging concepts: "I see something dark blue. I see something big that is blue."

When playing such games, it is good to keep your language at a simple level so the children can understand. But during family conversations, you can be more flexible. Let the children see that you enjoy using words and that you delight in discovering new words to add to your own vocabulary. If you show eagerness to explain the meanings of unfamiliar words, children will ask about words they do not recognize. They love to show they have learned new words.

Baby Talk

Baby talk is speech that is marked by substitution, omission, or addition of certain sounds. For example, young children frequently substitute *th* for *f* or *s*, *w* for *v*, and *t* for *c*.

Baby talk is normal. Children have to learn how to use their vocal mechanism, how to listen, and how to repeat the pronunciations they hear. Children progress at different rates, but most outgrow baby talk before the first grade. If your children use baby talk, do not criticize them or make them self-conscious. Use the same words, pronounced correctly but without drawing attention to them, in your conversation with them. The children will hear your pronunciations and soon will adopt them.

READING SKILLS

People learn to read by building on basic skills. Adults can forget how basic some of these skills are. For instance, a child learning to read English has to learn to go from left to right on a line.

When reading a book to young children, always begin with the front cover. Show that a book starts at the front and continues page by page to the end. Turn to the title page and read the title of the book and the name of the author.

As you read, run your finger under the words you say. This stresses the relationship between the printed marks and the words you are saying. It also shows that you are reading the print from left to right across the page and from top to bottom.

Here is an activity that will help launch a child toward reading. Make a book with your child. Cut pictures out of magazines and tape them onto sheets that can be stapled together. Put one picture on each page. Then ask the child to create a story about the pictures. Write the story under the pictures, one sentence for each picture. Make a cover for the book, complete with a title and your child's name as author. The first time you do this, the child may find it hard to come up with a story idea. Suggest an appropriate topic. Try something related to your child's experience, such as *Sara's Favorite Meal* or *James Goes to the Beach.*

Reading Aloud

One of the most important things parents can do is read to their children at least once a day. Reading is something you enjoy and something you want your children to enjoy. They will enjoy the stories and sharing the time with you.

Here are a few hints:

1. Evening is usually the best time to read, but do not limit reading to only a certain time.

2. Let the children see the words and pictures as you read.

3. Consider your children's attention spans. Young children usually have short attention spans, so keep readings short. As children grow, they will be able to sit attentively for longer periods of time.

4. Paying attention is an important skill for children to learn. Establish standards of conduct. Of course, children will wiggle or interrupt or just look at the pictures, but do not allow them to play with toys or do other things that distract their attention from the story you are reading.

Reading Comprehension

To make certain your children understand a story, ask appropriate questions, such as, What is the name of the girl in the story? What food does she like best?

After you read a story, have the children retell it while looking at the pictures in the book. Later, ask them to retell stories without looking at pictures. For instance, you might ask children to retell stories at the dinner table. If your children have been to a story hour at the local library that afternoon, ask them to tell about a story they heard.

As the children mature, ask their opinions about stories. Do you think this is a funny story? Would you like to do the same things the boy did in the story? How would you feel if this happened to you?

Another activity for maturing children is predicting what will happen next in a story. The best places to do this are at the end of a chapter and just before you turn the page. What do you think Anne will do? Will Stephen get there in time? Who is in the house? Who else? Why do you think they're in the house?

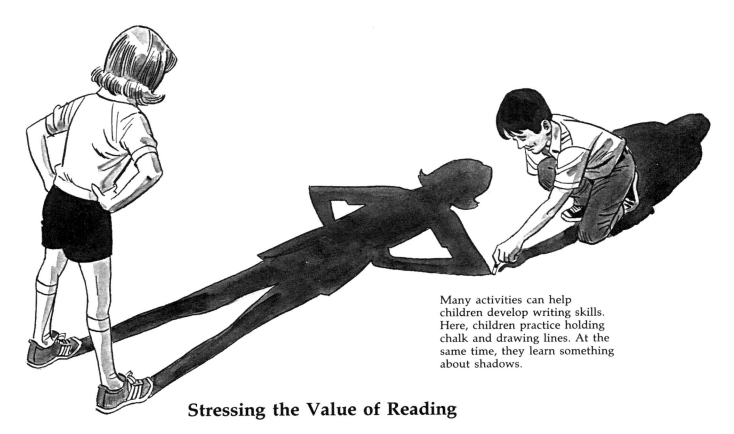

Many activities can help children develop writing skills. Here, children practice holding chalk and drawing lines. At the same time, they learn something about shadows.

Stressing the Value of Reading

From time to time, point out to your children the advantages of being able to read. Choose things that have immediate value to them. Do not stress that reading will enable them to get good grades or go to college or get a good job. Young children are not ready for such considerations.

Street signs have meaning because they are part of children's everyday world. Introduce them to STOP signs. Explain that this sign means drivers must stop their cars. What could happen if a driver could not read the sign? Do people who ride bikes also have to be able to read this sign? Why?

Let children see that knowing how to read enables you to find out the prices of merchandise in stores, the contents of cans and bottles, and the flavors of ice cream that are available. In restaurants you can learn what dishes are on the menu, and which containers hold salt and pepper. At the zoo you can learn the names of animals by reading signs.

Reading is also fun. It enables people to enjoy books and newspapers, including comics. Read comic strips to your children. They are good for learning to read from left to right. Look for odd and amusing news items to share with them—a circus elephant story, a picture and caption about a treed cat that had to be rescued, people bathing in the icy ocean on January first.

Help your children keep a list of things family members read in one day. Do not forget mail, posters in stores, medicine containers, text on the TV screen.

Learning the Alphabet

Children must learn that there are 26 letters in the alphabet and that our words are made up of these letters.

There is a time-honored way to teach letters—one at a time. Once children recognize a letter, they will eagerly look for it everywhere. Make looking for letters a game: Let's find ten boxes in the store that have the letter S on them. Circle ten S's in the newspaper. Circle ten words in the newspaper that begin with S.

Another good activity is making a letter scrapbook. Devote one or two pages to each letter. You and the children can go through newspapers and magazines and cut out examples of each letter as you teach them the letter. Also look for pictures of objects whose names begin with the letter. Put the letters and pictures together in the scrapbook.

Make an alphabet chart and hang it on a wall where children can see it easily. This helps familiarize your children with the order of the letters.

A package of magnetized plastic letters makes a good rainy-day present. Give the children a metal tray on which they can sort the letters and move them about. Have them put their favorite letters on the refrigerator door. Ask them to use the letters to copy words you print.

WRITING READINESS

In preparing children for writing, it is helpful to develop their hand muscles and eye-hand coordination. One way to do this is to encourage the use of puzzles, modeling clay, crayons, fingerpaints, and other materials that develop muscle control. Give them connect-a-dot pictures to complete. Show them how to make necklaces by stringing beads or dried macaroni. Let them practice using a key to lock and unlock doors. All these activities help develop manual skills needed for writing.

Help children develop an awareness of the purpose of writing. Let them watch you write for items in catalogs. Later, they will share in opening the packages. Print their names on their coats, artwork, and other belongings. Show them that not all stories are printed in books. Write a story while the children watch, then read it to them. When writing a letter to relatives, ask the children what they would like to say. Then let them watch you write down their words. When a letter from a relative arrives, read to the children the parts that pertain to them.

LEARNING TO PRINT

When teaching children how to print letters, it is not necessary to go in alphabetical order. Start with the first letter of the children's names or with letters that are easy to make, such as *I, L,* and *T.* The hardest to make usually are *Q, K,* and *R.*

Begin with capital letters and teach one letter at a time. Show the children how to make the strokes that form the letter. Give the children plenty of practice with that letter. Paper and pencils should be easily accessible to the children so they can write without having to ask you. And practice need not be limited to paper exercises. If you go to the beach, show them how to write large letters in the wet sand. If their writing consists of nothing but scribbles, do not object. Even scribbling is worthwhile.

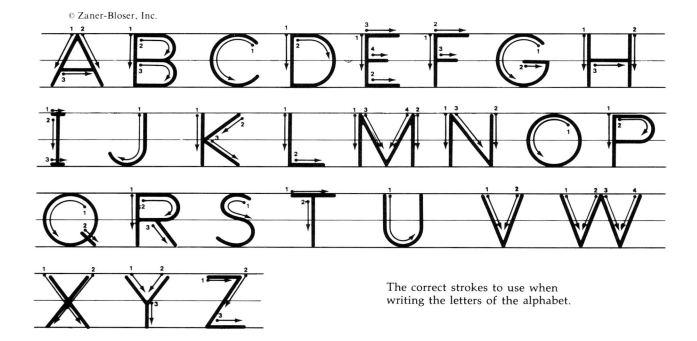

The correct strokes to use when writing the letters of the alphabet.

THINKING SKILLS

Two important prereading skills involve recognizing logical relationships between objects or events.

Same-Different

In order to read, children must be able to recognize and distinguish printed letters and words. A great variety of activities can be used to help develop the needed skills.

Cut out a large letter or other symbol, an *A* or a *$*, for example, and paste it at the top of a sheet of paper. Have the children find matching symbols, cut them out, and paste them on the sheet.

Teach children the names of shapes: squares, triangles, rectangles, circles, etc. Make a cardboard sample of each. Write the name of the shape on the sample. Tell the children the names and point out examples of each in your home.

Ask questions. How are you and your father alike? How are you different? How is a picnic supper different from supper at home? How are they the same? How is your jacket like mine? How is it different?

Ask the children to compare characters in stories they know: Mother Bear and Baby Bear in "Goldilocks and the Three Bears," Cinderella and her stepmother in "Cinderella." Ask them to compare characters from different stories, such as Cinderella and Snow White or Robin Hood and the Pied Piper.

Recognizing shapes and learning their names can be fun when parents turn learning into a game. Here, a parent names a shape and the child finds the shape in nearby objects.

Sorting

The ability to organize things into groups is based on the concept of same-different. Begin with two kinds of objects that are obviously different and ask the children to separate them so that all similar objects are together. Use pennies and buttons, clothespins and paper clips, nuts and bolts. Gradually increase the types of objects and the complexity of the task. Make the task useful. The children will feel proud that they have helped you. Ask them to sort nails and screws, forks and spoons, different colored buttons, different coins. Egg cartons are useful for sorting small objects.

Show that sorting can be done according to various standards. Buttons, for example, can be sorted according to color or size. Ask the children how they might sort their toys—board games, dolls, things that have wheels, things that make noise. Such sorting can be a good challenge.

During a walk, collect leaves. At home, have the children separate them into types. Later you can show them how to save the leaves by pressing them.

Classify words. Take turns listing size words: *big, gigantic, tiny;* happy words: *smile, grin, giggle;* taste words: *sweet, sour, hot, delicious;* and time words: *early, late, morning, tomorrow.*

Such activities encourage children to think without making impossible demands on them. Even when children have trouble completing the tasks, you will be helping them grow as long as you compliment them on successes and reassure them when they prove too young for a task. Wait some weeks and then try again. Little by little their achievements will increase.

Chapter Five

BEGINNING READERS

THE WORLD BECOMES DIFFERENT when children begin to read. No longer do they depend on you to tell them the meaning of every word, sign, or book title. They become eager to show you how well they read. Of course you are full of admiration. But you know that your children are just beginning to learn a complex task. Many skills still wait to be developed, and many hurdles lie ahead. You can help your children with these skills just as successfully as you can with prereading skills.

Continue many of the routines you established when the children were younger. Reading aloud should continue daily, but now you need not do all the reading. Many of the word games described in the previous chapter can still be entertaining. Just make them a bit more difficult. When classifying words, for example, provide more challenging categories, such as behavior words: *polite, rude, noisy, helpful;* hat words: *pretty, plain, waterproof;* or elephant words: *huge, heavy, massive, clumsy.*

Share the family reading of stories by encouraging your children to read the easy parts. Choose books with lots of words the children know so they are not frustrated by their early attempts at reading.

Suggest to relatives that they send occasional letters and post-cards to your children. Be enthusiastic when such mail arrives. Involve your children in the mail you receive, including mail that is part of everyday life, such as bills. Begin with a bill that is for

32

Involving grandparents in your children's intellectual development is rewarding for both generations.

something they are familiar with, such as clothing you bought for them; explain how to read the bill.

Share the daily newspaper with your children. Make reading the children's favorite comic strip a daily activity. Encourage them to read the easy parts. Read with them any articles that might interest them: the report of a baseball game, a local event, plans for a new swimming pool in town. Ask them to find the weather report and read it to you.

Play board and card games that involve reading and increase vocabulary. Many excellent games are available.

READING COMPREHENSION

As children learn to read, they may make excellent progress in saying the words printed on the page, but not in getting the meaning of what they read.

To strengthen your children's reading comprehension skills, continue to ask the kinds of questions you asked when they were younger and listening to you read aloud. Ask about things they have read themselves, both silently and aloud, and things you have read to them.

Interpreting Stories

Often, the most difficult books to comprehend are works of fiction. Have your children watch for these aspects of a story:

1. *Characters.* Who are the characters in the story? Tell me a little about them.

2. *Setting.* Where does the story take place? When does it take place? Is the setting important to the story?

3. *Plot.* What happens in the story?

4. *Theme.* What is the main idea of the story?

If children give answers that you think are incorrect, ask them to read aloud the part of the story on which their answers are based. If they have difficulty in answering one or more of the questions, look at the story with them to find the answers.

Follow up basic questions with more specific ones. Ask for details, such as a description of the main character's home. Ask children to make inferences; for example, What do you think will happen to the characters after the story ends? Ask for opinions of the story, the characters, and the characters' behavior. By learning to think about and discuss stories they read, your children will become more competent readers.

Sequencing

Another important reading skill is sequencing—putting things in proper order. After reading a story, ask children what happened first, second, . . . last. Cut apart the frames of a comic strip and shuffle their order. Have the children put them in the correct order. Scramble a sentence and have children put the words in the correct order. When you play Simon Says, give a series of directions and see if the children can follow the directions in the same order in which you gave them. As the children improve, add more directions or make the directions more complicated.

LEARNING TO RECOGNIZE WORDS

Sight Words

We learn some words as units rather than by sounding out the letters that make up the words. Words learned as units—that is, by the way they look—are called sight words. Even words that are learned by sounding out become sight words once we master them.

There are several reasons why some words are learned by the look-and-say method rather than by the sounding-out method. To begin with, for some beginning readers, it may be easier to learn words by sight than to learn the rules of sounding out. Secondly, many words cannot be sounded out easily, and may even seem to violate rules of sounding out. This is why words like *school, could,* and *know* are usually taught as sight words. Thirdly, knowing some words by sight makes it easier for children to analyze and sound out other words. They can be taught to see and hear similarities between the words they know and new words.

Most of the words in beginners' books are sight words. Help your children master them. Ask them to use the words in sentences. Write the words on flash cards for practice sessions you treat as a game. Praise every correct answer.

Expand your children's sight recognition vocabulary by helping them learn to read things in their environment: street signs, food packages, magazine names, clothing labels, toy advertisements, etc.

Phonics

It is not possible to learn every word by sight. To become effective readers, children must learn how to sound out new words that they meet in their reading. They will find it useful to break words into syllables, sound out each syllable, then put the words back together again. This study of the relationship between letters and sounds is called phonics.

Most experts recommend that parents leave the teaching of phonics to the schools. There are many rules to learn, and there can be much confusion because some letters and letter combinations have two or more different sounds. Consider, for instance, the sounds made by *g* in *giant* and *green* and the sounds made by *ch* in *children, choir,* and *chef.*

MORE WORD GAMES

Opposites. What's the opposite of . . .? Use adjectives that are part of your children's listening and speaking vocabularies: *slow, fast, soft, noisy, loud.*

Tell me what's different. Give four words, three of which are related; for example: *red, green, boat, pink.* Children have to tell which word does not belong and why.

Riddles. Kids love riddles, and there are hundreds. Here are some starters: What goes up every time that rain comes down? An umbrella. What has 18 legs and catches flies? A baseball team. What always goes to sleep with shoes on? A horse.

BUILDING VOCABULARY

Continue the efforts to expand vocabulary that you used when your children were younger. Show them that many words are made up of two smaller words. These are called compound words. *Birthday, playhouse, everywhere, snowball, downstairs,* and *airplane* are examples. Have the children make a list of compound words. Post it on the refrigerator. Encourage the children to continue to add words to the list. If they get stuck, suggest they look around the house. *Pancake, applesauce,* and *bedroom* are a few of the things they will find.

As they begin to read, children will be introduced to contractions. To make certain they understand what the contractions represent, give them practice. Say a sentence that contains a contraction and ask children to say it without the contraction. *I'll* buy a pink petunia. *I will* buy a pink petunia. He *didn't* like pancakes. He *did not* like pancakes. *We're* making lemonade. *We are* making lemonade.

Many words are changed by adding endings such as *-ed, -ing, -est,* and *-er.* Have children circle words in newspapers that have these endings. Talk about how these endings change the meaning of a word and how the words are used: Mary *invited* me to her party, Mary *is inviting* me, etc.

Children often can use help with plural nouns. Most words are made plural by adding *s* or *es.* But some words undergo a major spelling change when they become plural: *goose–geese, mouse–mice, child–children, foot–feet.* Have children circle plural nouns in newspaper articles and point out plurals on roadside signs.

Have children name different kinds of objects, such as makes of cars, names of trees, birds, or vegetables. Add one or two items to their lists if you can.

WHAT RHYMES WITH. . .?

Rhyming activities help children learn to listen carefully. For example, ask children to name five words that rhyme with *pat* or with *man.* Can they name an object that rhymes with *run* or an animal that rhymes with *big?* Together, read some poems that rhyme. Have the children point out the rhyming words. Encourage children to make up their own rhyming poems.

ALPHABETIZING

Being able to put words in alphabetical order is an essential skill; it enables children to use all sorts of reference materials, from the index at the back of a book to dictionaries, encyclopedias, and telephone directories. Thus, it is important to give children practice in alphabetizing.

Start with two words that begin with different letters of the alphabet, then progress to three and four words: *cat, lion, bear, elephant.* After they have mastered these, present words that begin with the same letter but have different second letters: *bear, bat, bull, boar;* then different third letters: *elevator, elbow, elm, elf,* and so on. This activity also helps develop concentration. If you are encouraged to give children lots of words to alphabetize, cut out words from newspaper headlines and paste each word on a 3-by-5 card. Begin with a few words, then add more as the children become proficient.

Help children create a telephone book listing—in alphabetical order—of the names and telephone numbers of their friends. Ask children to look up telephone numbers for you in your address book and, when they are ready, in the telephone directory.

WRITING SKILLS

It is important to provide activities that let children practice their writing skills and that demonstrate to them how useful writing is. For example, it is good to encourage them to write to grandparents and other relatives. Such notes can be short additions to your letters or they can be separate communications that will also give them practice in writing addresses. If you and the children take a trip to an interesting place, suggest that they write postcards to relatives and friends. Even "Hello! Love, Pat" is a worthy achievement for a beginning writer.

Watch newspapers and magazines for booklets, posters, free samples, and other things you and your children can send for. There are several books that list hundreds of free items children can request. Encourage your children to write for items that interest them.

To help ensure that letters are not written in vain, look over each offer with the children to make certain they have followed directions. For instance, some companies require people to enclose a self-addressed envelope. Also check to see if there are any charges they overlooked.

Make a habit of leaving notes for your children to read: Do you want to go swimming with me tomorrow? I made lemonade for you. Please give the dog some water. Note writing shows children you are thinking about them. It also shows them that writing is a useful way to pass on information. Finally, it helps get them into the habit of following written directions. In your notes, use words your children understand, print clearly, and post the notes where they will see them.

The purpose of all this is to encourage your children to write, write, write and read, read, read.

WHAT'S HAPPENING IN SCHOOL?

Your children will benefit if you take an interest in everything that goes on in school. Ask them what they did in school today and listen attentively to whatever they choose to discuss, whether it is a science experiment or a baseball game. Ask relevant questions. Also ask questions on other aspects of their day: Did you enjoy the spelling bee? Did you play with the hamster? What did Julie bring to show and tell? But do not turn your questions into a daily report card. You must show interest without appearing to be checking up.

Let the children's teachers know you are interested. Attend open houses and parent-teacher conferences. Do not be reluctant to make appointments with teachers if you are concerned about your children's progress.

HEALTH CONSIDERATIONS

Healthy children lead active lives—at play, at school, and at home —and parents have the responsibility of seeing to it that their children are in good health. For this reason, parents arrange for regular dental examinations for each child; they see to it that children are immunized against childhood diseases; and they arrange for periodic physical examinations.

Of particular importance for reading and learning are good vision and hearing. Many children require eyeglasses in order to see well enough to read and learn effectively. While schools may offer eye examinations for children entering school, as children grow, changes in vision may occur, and often rather rapidly. Teachers and parents must be alert to signs of poor vision in school-age children. Some of these signs are squinting, headaches, lack of interest in school, and listlessness. If you have any reason to suspect that your children may need eyeglasses, do not hesitate to consult a health professional.

Poor hearing is more difficult to detect by laymen and so can easily be ignored if parents and teachers are not alert. A child who does not hear perfectly may be thought of as being below average in intelligence, uninterested in school, or surly. Again, as with possible problems of vision, parents should see to it that such matters are brought to the attention of the appropriate health professional.

38

Chapter Six

INDEPENDENT READERS

THE WAY TO BECOME A GOOD READER is to read a great deal. So, when children are put off by the idea of reading on their own, you might suggest that they try reading aloud to you. It is vital that they read. Good subjects for such reading are the picture books or Mother Goose stories you read to them when they were younger. They may say those stories are too babyish, but in most cases the idea will appeal to them, since they usually remember the stories fondly. If they do resist the suggestion, you might ask them to read the stories aloud to a younger brother or sister. Such practice is a good way to overcome reluctance to read.

As time goes by, many of the activities introduced earlier should become routine: asking children about their day in school, playing word games and doing puzzles with them, having them write letters and notes to relatives. Continue to build reading comprehension skills by asking specific questions about the books they read. After you read a book together, discuss it informally. The complexity of your questions should increase gradually as the children improve.

Because you will want to reinforce and build on the materials taught in school, it is essential to remain knowledgeable about the school curriculum. Keep in touch with your children's teachers. If the school permits, ask children to bring home the textbooks they use. Read the books yourself. Look over homework assignments. Review tests and other papers they bring home, remembering to praise work done well. For instance, a good spelling mark can be displayed on a kitchen bulletin board for others to admire. Take care not to hurt the feelings of a child who may be having trouble in school.

FOLLOW ME!

A wonderful family activity is to read plays aloud, with each member of the family taking a role. This can be fun, and it gives children a chance to practice using vocal variety and other speaking skills. It is an activity that can be continued right through high school and even beyond, as your children progress toward the great works of dramatic literature.

SILENT READING

Mastering silent reading involves many of the skills children use in oral reading, but differences in children's habits can result in greatly differing levels of comprehension. Some children may skip over difficult words when they read silently. Other children may have trouble in concentrating on silent reading.

It is easiest for children to pay attention to their reading when material interests them. But even motivated readers should be questioned about what they have read, to make sure they have good understanding.

Set aside some time almost every day for silent reading. Begin with 15-minute periods and, as the practice takes hold, gradually expand reading time to 30 minutes or more. Be a good model. While your children are reading silently, you should be enjoying a book or magazine of your own. And if the children begin quizzing you on your reading comprehension, answer their questions. If you speak enthusiastically about what you have read, they may want to read it themselves.

Other Reading Is Important

Continue to read aloud with your children, preferably with the entire family present. Children who can read by themselves still enjoy cuddling up to parents and hearing a good story. Listening builds listening skills and gives children a chance to use their imaginations. Choose stories that have slightly higher reading levels than those the children feel confident about tackling alone. This will help them grow in reading.

Also continue to ask your children to read aloud to you. Listen to their pronunciation. Many words look or sound alike: *tired–tried, quiet–quite, desert–dessert, mouth–month.* If children do not read such words correctly, they may miss the meaning of what they are reading. Comprehension also is helped through good phrasing and inflection as the children read.

Help them with hard words. Give them a few seconds to try pronouncing words on their own. If they cannot, pronounce the words for them and let them go on with the story. Do your best to keep the activity enjoyable.

USING READING SKILLS

Continue to give your children opportunities to use written materials in their everyday lives. For example, ask them to read to you the words on the jackets of their favorite record albums or the listing of programs to be shown on television over the weekend. Show them how to read and understand the ingredients and nutritional information on food packages.

If children are at home when the mail arrives, encourage them to open letters addressed to Occupant and tell you what they contain. Ask them to look through advertising from supermarkets to see if the stores have a sale on foods you need. Look over telephone and electric bills with the children. Show them how to read the bills. Point out items they will understand, such as long-distance telephone calls to relatives.

Children love catalogs, especially the toy sections. At first, they are attracted by the pictures. It is up to you to show them that to understand what is being offered they have to read the accompanying text. When they find a toy they like, ask them how big it is, what it is made of, whether it has to be assembled, whether batteries are needed, whether the price includes postage and handling. If necessary, help them find the answers to such questions. Let them help you as you order things from seed, clothing, and other catalogs.

Making a collection of misspelled signs on restaurants and shops helps build reading, spelling, and observation skills.

Keep a supply of books, magazines, and newspapers, including publications designed for your children's age group. Consider subscribing to at least one children's magazine, such as *Ranger Rick, Cobblestone,* or *3-2-1 Contact.*

Encourage your children to read the newspaper every day. You might have each child read one comic strip to the entire family just

42

after a meal. It should be a strip everyone in the family enjoys. Make discussions of the news part of your family conversations. Of course, the items discussed should be appropriate for children. If you talk about news from faraway places, use a map to show the children where the events are taking place. Point out news articles that relate to children's interests, for example, in sports, fashion, or computers. Choose activities that require children to read articles. For instance, ask a sports-minded child to keep a scrapbook about sports. If your newspaper has essay, drawing, or other contests for children, encourage your children to take part in them.

Following Directions

Being able to follow written directions is an essential skill. It is needed to do homework and take tests, learn to play a new game and do a science experiment, make a dress, and build a model ship. And it is needed in all sorts of adult activities, from fixing a leaky faucet to finding the way to a friend's house.

An excellent way to help boys and girls to develop their ability to follow written directions is to involve them in cooking. With the children's agreement, select a simple recipe. Begin by reading the list of ingredients, one item at a time. Either have the children read while you gather the ingredients or, if the children's reading skills are not strong enough, do the reading while they gather the items. Next, help them read through all the steps in the recipe. Define any words they do not understand. Then follow the steps. Let the children do as much of the work as possible.

Fine cookbooks have been written especially for children. Buy one as a gift or borrow it from the library. Once a week, encourage your children to cook for a family meal.

Give your children other opportunities to follow written instructions. Let them read the instructions as you put together an object you have purchased unassembled. If a new shirt has to be cleaned, ask them to read the instructions on the label. When introducing a new activity, go over the instructions with your children. Many products come with poorly written or insufficient directions, leading to frustration even among skilled readers.

BUILDING VOCABULARY

Continue to play word games as you do chores, take car trips, and so on. Use games described earlier or make up new ones. How many words can we list that contain a double r ? For example, *arrive, carriage, furry, mirror, parrot.* Take turns adding words to the list. You might ask one of the children to write down all the words. Variations include making lists of words that end with an *o,* that begin with a certain prefix, that end with a certain suffix, that contain *ant (plant, giant, cantaloupe)* and so on.

To help children use prefixes correctly, name a word and have them add a prefix: *appear–disappear, friendly–unfriendly, patient–impatient, convenient–inconvenient.* Then use the children's words in sentences. Reverse the process, with the children giving words, determining if you added the correct prefix, and using your words in sentences.

Name an adjective and have the children give a noun that goes with the adjective: *funny, clown; old, shoe.* Give a noun and ask for an appropriate adjective.

Provide practice with synonyms and antonyms. Say a word and ask children to give synonyms or antonyms for that word. Or say a sentence and ask the children to change one word to give the sentence the opposite meaning:

I am very *tall.* (I am very *short.*)
I *bought* a baseball. (I *sold* a baseball.)
The army *attacked* the fort. (The army *defended* the fort.)

Encourage your children to write thank-you letters, get-well notes, party invitations, pen-pal letters, and other correspondence.

44

HOMONYMS

Homonyms sound alike but are spelled differently and have different meanings.

Take turns with your children making up sentences that include homonyms. For example:

When I was sick I was *weak* for a *week.*
Our mother went shopping for an *hour.*
The *knight* escaped at *night.*

Here are some common homonyms:

air, ere, heir	hoarse, horse	real, reel
altar, alter	hole, whole	sail, sale
ate, eight	knew, new	scene, seen
bare, bear	knot, not	sea, see
beat, beet	mail, male	seam, seem
buy, by, bye	main, mane	shone, shown
capital, capitol	meat, meet	soar, sore
cents, scents, sense	oar, or, ore	some, sum
cite, sight, site	one, won	stake, steak
dew, do, due	pale, pail	their, there, they're
die, dye	peace, piece	threw, through
fair, fare	plain, plane	to, too, two
flour, flower	pray, prey	toe, tow
grate, great	principal, principle	wail, whale
hear, here	rain, reign, rein	ware, wear, where
heard, herd	read, reed	wood, would

CONVERSATIONAL SKILLS

Give your children time to speak and be listened to each day. Ask questions that stimulate their minds and touch off further conversation. An effective parent does lots of listening and quite a bit of talking.

Remember, your children will imitate your speech patterns, so use good sentence structure and grammar. It is easy to become a lazy speaker—to use *thing* instead of the specific name of an object, to use the latest slang words. Without discouraging your children's desire to talk with you, help them to resist such habits. If they tell you a book is *cool,* ask whether they mean it is interesting or beautiful or funny or exciting or any of many other words.

Some conversations require the use of writing. Show children how to take telephone messages. This is also good practice for taking accurate notes. Have them make shopping lists and invitation lists for parties. When in the supermarket, have the children check items off on the shopping list.

THREE GAMES FOR CREATIVE THINKING

1001 Uses. Take turns with your children thinking up practical uses for a common object, such as a tin can, pencil, book, or blanket. Accept all reasonable suggestions, but ask for explanations if you do not understand a child's reasoning.

What's the Question? Give an answer. Ask the children to provide an appropriate question. Then reverse roles.

On the kitchen table. (Where did I leave the book?)

The dog barked. (Why did the burglar run away?)

Florida. (Where does grandma live?)

Brainstormers. Make a list of all the items you and your children can think of in a category. Have a child write down the items as they are named. If necessary, help with spelling. Here are some categories.

clothing	things made of glass	capitals
furniture	things that have handles	road signs
fruits	things that can be heard	explorers
birds	parts of the body	presidents
sports	home appliances	scientists

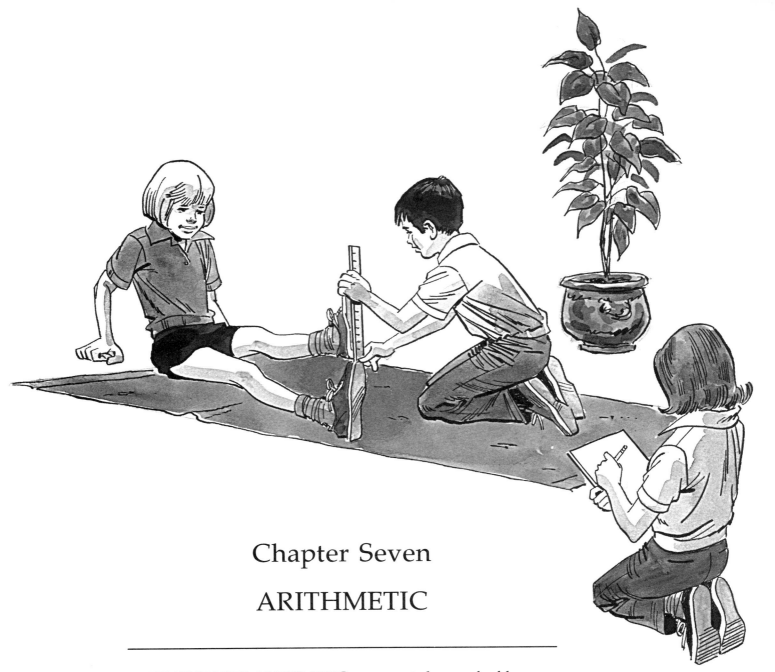

Chapter Seven

ARITHMETIC

EVERYONE USES ARITHMETIC—to count change, double a recipe, balance a checkbook, divide a pizza, determine how much someone has grown in the past year. Arithmetic is the science of numbers. Understanding the meaning of numbers and how numbers are used requires a degree of maturity. Children are usually not ready to learn simple arithmetic until they are six or seven years old. Before this, however, children can be introduced to activities that involve thinking in mathematical terms.

As with language arts skills, you can best help your children master arithmetic skills if you begin early and continue through the school years.

LEARNING TO COUNT

Children generally learn to count long before they understand the meaning of counting. They can recite the numbers from one to ten, but have no idea what the numbers mean. Use many different objects when teaching numbers. Show the children one finger, one spoon, one raisin; then two fingers, two spoons, two raisins. Gradually move up to 10, then to 20.

Make a number book using colored paper squares, stickers, dry macaroni, or other objects. At the top of each page, write a number. Have children paste the correct number of items on each page. Later, ask them to create a number book by drawing the correct number of items on each page.

Look for numbers around your home and on walks through town. Children will discover that numbers are everywhere: on house doors, supermarket signs, mileage signs, buses, gasoline pumps, and so on.

As you teach children numbers, you can also get them accustomed to comparing amounts: more-less, bigger-smaller, heavier-lighter. In a supermarket, pick up two bunches of grapes and ask which has more grapes. In a zoo, ask which of two animals weighs more. At home, have children compare the sizes of two rooms or two dishes.

Encourage children to put things into groups: three buttons, two carrots. Ask how many groups of four they can make with objects in the kitchen: spoons, forks, dried beans, raisins, napkins. Then have them put away one item from each group. How big are the groups that remain?

Use numbers in conversation. This helps children understand what numbers mean and how people use them. Let them hear you counting apples in the supermarket, socks in the laundromat, books you borrow from the library. Give the children instructions and ask them questions: Take one onion out of the bag. Put four spoons on the table. How many letters did we receive?

Play games such as May I? In this game one person gives instructions, such as, "Take 3 steps to the right" or "Skip forward two times." In this game, children may do so only if they first ask, "May I?" All your directions should gradually lead the children to a hidden orange or other treat.

Many other games help build number recognition and counting skills. Spend an evening now and then playing rummy, bingo, or games such as Sorry and Parchesi. Bingo is particularly useful in helping children learn to identify and pronounce two-digit numbers such as 27 and 43.

MEASURING

By first grade, children are ready to be introduced to rulers, yardsticks, and measuring tapes. Show how these objects are divided into inches. Show how long 1 inch is, and point out that an inch is always exactly the same length.

Do some measuring. Measure the length of everyone's T-shirts or how far the children can throw a ball. Then let the children explore your home with rulers and tapes. Ask them the length in inches of a loaf of bread, a spoon, the daily newspaper. Ask them who has the widest bed, the biggest beach towel, the shortest chair. Let the children measure how tall they are, the length of their feet, the distance around their wrists. Show your children how to use a scale to determine how much they weigh. Let them watch as you weigh produce in a store.

Introduce measuring cups and spoons. How much milk does a drinking glass hold? Hold many tablespoons of water equal a cup of water? Show the children recipes in a cookbook, and discuss why measuring items is important in cooking and baking.

Metrics

Many elementary schools introduce children to the metric system of measurement. The metric system seems difficult to most Americans because we are accustomed to thinking in terms of feet, pounds, and gallons—the English system—instead of in meters, grams, and liters. Point out to your children that many products sold in the United States list weight in both English and metric units. Reference books frequently use both systems. For example, a book may state: "The highest point in South Carolina is Sassafras Mountain, which has an elevation of 3560 feet (1086 meters)."

Purchase a measuring stick that shows both English and metric units. Have children use both systems to conduct various measurements around the house: the perimeter of their beds, the area of a rug, the length of the bathtub. If you have a kitchen scale that shows both English and metric units, design similar activities involving ounces and grams. Help children see how easy it is to convert grams to kilograms.

Temperature

Show children how to read a thermometer. Explain the significance of its ups and downs by associating temperature with what happens in the environment. What happens to water when the temperature drops below 32 degrees? When the temperature rises above 32 degrees?

Introduce older children to Celsius thermometers. Point out that on the Celsius scale, the freezing point of water is 0 degrees, and the boiling point is 100 degrees, much easier to remember than 32 degrees and 212 degrees Fahrenheit. Consider purchasing a thermometer that shows both scales. At breakfast each morning, announce the temperature in one scale and ask children to guess what it is in the other scale.

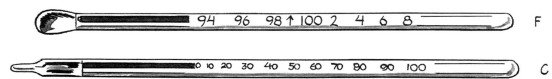

Measuring skills can be taught by using thermometers, yardsticks, rulers, measuring cups, and other common household items.

REINFORCING ARITHMETIC

Most schools have similar objectives for the math skills children in each grade should be taught. At the beginning of each school year, examine your children's math textbooks to find out what they will be learning during the coming year. Throughout the year, look at their homework to learn what they are studying at the moment. Find activities that will help school learning.

For instance, when children are learning fractions, have them help allocate portions of food among family members. Ask them to cut an apple in quarters, a banana in half.

THE VALUE OF MONEY

Deciding how to spend 25 cents is not easy but children enjoy the chance to buy something on their own. They are using concepts such as equal, more than, and less than and are learning that money management is a matter of making choices. In short, they are developing self-reliance and are using reading and math skills.

By the time children are three or four, they understand that money buys things. Let them hand the money to the cashier when you purchase a book or toy.

When the children have learned to count, identify various coins and discuss their value. Explain that five pennies equal one nickel, that ten equal a dime, that two nickels equal one dime. Play a trading game: "I'll give you a nickel. How many pennies should you give me?"

Find opportunities to mention the cost of common items, such as toys, food, and clothing. Point out the price tags on items in a store and explain that the cost of items influences your buying decisions. When a child asks you to buy raspberries, you may explain that you are buying apples instead because they are less expensive. Show how many apples you can buy for the same price as a box of raspberries. When a child asks you to buy a toy, you might say that you are saving money so the family can have a picnic on Saturday.

Giving young children money to spend as they wish helps teach them the value of money and encourages the use of reading and math skills.

Allowances

By the age of five or six, children should receive regular weekly allowances. Start with a small amount. As the children get older and their real needs for money increase, allowances should be increased accordingly.

When you begin giving children allowances, point out that this is the only spending money you will normally provide. If they choose to spend it all within an hour of receiving it, fine. But they should not expect to receive additional spending money during the week.

Discuss with them what the allowances are expected to cover. At first, when allowances are small, you may wish to let children spend the money any way they want. But even at this time, you should point out the advantages of saving some of the money so they can purchase more desirable, more expensive items.

As allowances grow, so should responsibilities. Many experts suggest that allowances be divided into money to spend, money to save, and money to share through birthday presents, contributions, etc. Be sure you and your children agree on what the allowance is expected to cover. Help them learn to budget their spending money, especially if it is supposed to cover school supplies, bus fares, and other essentials. Open a savings account in a local bank for them.

Mistakes will occur. If children spend all their money on toys and then tell you they have no money for school lunches, sit down and discuss with them how to solve this problem, and how to prevent it in the future.

Sometimes, children will have needs that cannot be covered by their allowances. Let them know you are always willing to discuss these with them. For instance, if children want new bicycles, you might agree to pay half the cost if they save the rest. Or you might pay children to do special jobs around the house. Children appreciate the value of a purchase more when they earn the money to pay for it themselves.

Always pay allowances on time, and never use money to bribe children. Do not threaten to withhold an allowance if a child misbehaves. Do not promise extra money if the child gets better grades. Such actions may teach wrong values to children.

Chapter Eight

SCIENCE, SOCIAL STUDIES, MUSIC, AND ART

ONE OF THE GREATEST assets of young children is their curiosity. They are eager to investigate and examine every new thing they encounter. It is important that you encourage children in their explorations of the world in which they live.

Asking what, why, how, where, and when is central to much of your children's behavior and conversation. Why is the sky blue? How do plants grow? Why does boiling water bubble? There is no way you can know the answers to all these questions. What is important is that you are interested in your children's questions and eager to help them find answers.

If you do not know the answer to a question, suggest that you find the answer together, either by asking someone who may know or by looking in an appropriate book. For older children, suggest that they find the answer themselves and tell you what they learned. Let them know you think the question is worthwhile. Sometimes children ask, "What would happen if . . .?" Encourage them to experiment and find out. Of course, you also should ask such questions of them: What happens if you bring the snowball into the house? If you put it in the freezer? After it melts, can you turn it back into snow?

SCIENCE SKILLS

Science is a method, a way of asking questions, looking at things, and trying to find out how and why things are the way they are. Do not concentrate on teaching facts to young children. Rather, give them opportunities to examine nature.

Activities with Animals

In learning to care for the family bird, fish, dog, or cat, your children will learn about the needs of living things: food, water, and a place to live. They will discover that all pets have characteristic behavioral patterns. And they will learn about birth, death, and the cycle of life.

Wherever you live, there are wild birds. Children can learn much by watching birds and listening to their calls. Build a feeder and stock it with seed. Take walks through various types of habitats. You will see different birds in a forest than in a meadow or on a sandy beach. Buy a guidebook that describes the birds living in your area and use it with your children to identify your bird visitors.

Activities with Plants

Show your children that leaves have different shapes. Help them learn to use leaves to identify plants. Point out that bark, flowers, and other parts of a plant also can be used for identification. When you take walks through a park, carry a plant guide. Show your children how to make bark and leaf rubbings. All you need are paper and crayons.

Keep a diary of changes in the garden. At first, you can write down what the children describe. Later, let the children keep the diary. Grow houseplants. Let your children be responsible for caring for them. Children particularly like plants with colorful leaves and flowers. Your guidance is important. For example, children may forget to water plants or may overwater them.

Conduct experiments with plants. What happens if a potted plant is placed on its side for a few days? What happens if you put a potato or the top of a carrot or pineapple in a dish of water?

A magnifying glass is an excellent gift for children. With it they can examine molds on stale bread, veins on a leaf, a tiny crab scurrying across the beach, and hundreds of other living things.

Caring for an animal develops a sense of responsibility and stimulates questions, forming the basis of a great deal of learning.

Learning About Physical Phenomena

Weather is one of the first aspects of the physical world that children are aware of. Make a point of commenting on the weather and how it affects what you wear or do that day. On a rainy day, place a pot outdoors to catch the rain. How much water falls during an hour? Overnight? Look at clouds and discuss how their shapes change. What clouds are seen on sunny days? Rainy days?

Cooking, mentioned elsewhere as a good activity to develop reading skills, also provides opportunities to learn some scientific principles. For instance, by preparing fruit-flavored drinks, children can learn about solutions. What happens to the powder when it is mixed with water? Can it be separated from the water by pouring the solution through a strainer?

Give your children a large magnet and a collection of nails, paper clips, and other iron-containing objects plus some nonmagnetic objects. Explain what a magnet is and let them experiment with it. (CAUTION: Keep magnets away from computers.)

When children are taking their baths, let them discover that certain things float and other things sink, that sponges and some other objects absorb water, that water takes the shape of its container, and so on.

SOCIAL STUDIES SKILLS

Children should learn gradually that they live in groups, and that there are great differences among people in a group—differences in their homes, clothes, occupations, foods, and customs. Using stories, walks, and discussions, let children learn that people live in many different kinds of homes. In your community, children may see that people live in houses, apartments, or trailers. Using trips to museums and pictures in books, you can show children other types of homes.

Help your children learn about the work that people do. Point out the work being done by store cashiers, butchers, road pavers, bank tellers, and so on. If you work outside the home, have the children visit your place of work and see what you do. If you are a full-time homemaker, point out the responsibilities of your work.

Celebrate holidays. Explain the meaning and historical significance of the holidays. Explain that some people celebrate different holidays than you do because they have different religious beliefs or because they live in different countries. If you or the children's grandparents came to the United States from another country, discuss some of the ways that people in that country celebrate holidays. Prepare a special dish served in the country.

Take every opportunity to interest young children in history and distant lands. Many fine books are available that bring the people of other times and places to life. Living museums, where life of days gone by is recreated, are excellent places to take children. Share with your children postcards and letters written by relatives and friends in foreign countries. Show them the stamps, explaining that all countries have their own stamps.

Map Magic

Maps are fascinating sources of information. The first map you introduce to your children might be a map of your community. It could even be a map you draw yourself. Use it when you take a walk. Let the children see how the map duplicates the real world. If you want, add landmarks to the map: your home, the post office, a favorite store or park.

Older children will enjoy looking at state and country maps. Spend time with them looking for unusual names, such as Lulu, Florida; Hi Hat, Kentucky; and Turkey, Texas. Have them keep a list of places with certain kinds of names, such as those of occupations (Bishop, Texas; Farmersville, California) or foods (Sugar City, Idaho; Pie, West Virginia). Your older children will enjoy looking for similarities between names of U.S. and foreign places. Have them find places in the United States that are named after places elsewhere: Bethlehem, Pennsylvania; Rome, New York; Peru, Indiana; Glasgow, Kentucky.

Play Capitals. Ask your children to name the capital of a state, let them ask you one, and so on. Progress to capitals of countries. Build a city alphabet. Starting with the letter A, name a city for each letter of the alphabet. The game gets more difficult if you limit cities to those in the United States.

Taking part in cleanups and other community improvement projects builds valuable citizenship skills.

Building Citizenship

Parents should be excellent examples of citizenship. Remember, you are your children's most important teacher. Do not set higher standards for them than you do for yourself. Obey laws, participate in community improvement projects, familiarize yourself with the news, vote in elections, and in other ways demonstrate the importance you attach to your role in the world in which you live. Your children will follow the example you set.

Music provides many opportunities for children to express themselves creatively. It also helps build important listening skills.

MUSICAL ACTIVITIES

Music should be part of your family's activities. Sing songs to your children and, when they are ready, teach them to sing the songs. Play rhythm games, asking your children to imitate you as you tap out a rhythm on a toy drum or other instrument. Encourage children to dance to music. This shows them that they can use their bodies to express feelings and ideas. How would they move to a march? A waltz? How would they act out a familiar song?

Make instruments with your children. They will enjoy playing with them and will learn basic concepts of music making. It is easy to make a rattle from a container, pebbles, acorns, nuts and bolts, or other small objects. And there are many different kinds of rattles to make. A can containing a few pebbles makes different sounds than a box containing a few pebbles or a box containing acorns.

Music involves an important skill often overlooked in other

areas: listening. Listen to records with your children. If you have a piano or other musical instrument, show your children how it is played. If possible, let them hear how different instruments make sounds. Record their singing so they can hear themselves.

Provide opportunities at home to listen to the classics as well as to modern music of high quality. You might consider playing quiet music during dinner or while you are doing a puzzle or craft with your children.

ART SKILLS

Children enjoy drawing, cutting, molding, mixing, scribbling, weaving—in short, doing anything artistic. Provide crayons, paints, modeling clay, chalk, mud, sand, yarns, pipe cleaners, plaster, or any of dozens of other materials and ask them to make something. Encourage your children to draw. At first (ages two to three), they will produce only scribbles. When they seem ready, you might show them how to draw a vertical line and a horizontal line. When they have mastered these, show them how to draw other shapes.

When children create something, ask them about it. What does it mean? Do they like it? And do not criticize a drawing because it is not perfect. Display your children's drawings and other art projects in a prominent place in your home. Occasionally suggest that they send a picture to their grandparents. This recognition of talents is very important.

Suggested Activities

Activities are limited only by imagination. Turn thumbprints into little figures and animals. Paint flat stones gathered at the beach, turning them into paperweights. Make collages with pictures from magazines, different kinds of seeds and rice, or old greeting cards. Turn a paper plate into a mask. Glue a tongue depressor or popsicle stick onto the bottom for use as a handle. Never hesitate to join in yourself.

Place a large sheet of paper on the floor and have your child lie on it. Trace around the child's body. Then let the child draw in eyes and other details with crayons. There you have it: a life-size portrait. If you have two or more children, let them trace one another.

When children are drawing or working with modeling clay, help them think of new things to create. If you could invent a new car, how would it look? How do you think creatures from outer space might look?

Chapter Nine

PROBLEMS IN LEARNING

POURING MILK FROM A CONTAINER into a glass is difficult for a child to do correctly. So is cutting a pie into equal portions. So is reading. All these skills must be learned, and during the learning process parents can expect children to make mistakes.

Parents also must remember that some children are eager and able to read at age five, but others are not ready until they are six or more. Some quickly master motor skills such as drawing and lettering. For others, these skills take much time and effort to learn. In addition, each child has strengths and weaknesses. Some children have lovely voices while others, though equally enthusiastic singers, appear to be tone deaf. Some children talk about nothing but horses. Others prefer sitting in front of a computer.

All these types of behavior are perfectly normal. But sometimes children fall far behind other children of the same age in the development of important skills. They may be excellent at arithmetic but unable to read. They may consistently miss the glass when pouring milk. They may have difficulty in understanding what is said to them. Do not ignore such problems but do not jump to conclusions. Yes, it is possible that the children are experiencing problems that require professional help. But it is also possible that simple changes in a child's environment will correct the situation.

MY CHILD AS A LEARNER

How do parents determine whether children have learning problems? There is no simple list of signs, no typical pattern of behavior. However, problems generally show themselves in one of three ways:

1. Children may have difficulty in developing language and thinking skills. They may appear to have trouble expressing ideas, or not be able to comprehend things they hear and read.

2. Children may have poor depth perception or difficulty in seeing or hearing.

3. Children may exhibit undesirable behavior. They may be overly aggressive, moody, or excessively shy. They may have physical symptoms, such as headaches, stomach aches, or excessive fatigue and listlessness.

Even if such signs are apparent, they may not signal the need for professional assistance. First, you might check out some other possibilities. For example:

● Do children have difficulty in hearing what is said because there is too much noise or other distractions in the home? Do they have difficulty understanding people who do not speak clearly?

● Do children spend hour after hour in front of the television set instead of reading, playing, and speaking with others? Children may not master learning skills unless they practice these skills.

● Do children get enough sleep? If they are allowed to stay up late, they will be tired at school and lack the energy and enthusiasm needed to learn.

● Do they eat properly? There is much evidence that nutrition plays a role in mental and physical development.

● Are the children moody and irritable because they do not receive enough of their parents' love and attention? Feelings of insecurity often can cause learning problems.

● Are the children nervous or withdrawn because there is too much pressure on them to succeed—either at home or at school? It is not uncommon for children to avoid making an effort because they are afraid of failure. They may avoid reading aloud or participating in discussions because they are afraid they will be ridiculed or told they are stupid. By letting children know that making mistakes is normal, they will feel comfortable about discussing their mistakes and how to correct them.

● Do children exhibit undesirable behavior primarily when they have to leave for school or after coming home from school? If so, a problem may exist in the classroom or on the school bus.

COMMON CAUSES OF LEARNING DIFFICULTIES

The most common causes of learning difficulties that require professional help are:

1. Medical problems, such as poor vision, impaired hearing, allergies, or glandular malfunctions.

2. Neurological disorders that interfere with the ability to handle symbols, whether heard or seen. Dyslexia is probably the most discussed neurological problem. A dyslexic person has difficulty in learning to read because of a tendency to reverse the letters of words, reverse letters themselves, or perceive words upside down or backwards. The dyslexic may read *pan* for *nap* or *u* for *n* or *710* for *oil.* Although a tendency toward reversals and upside-down viewing is common among beginning readers, most children soon outgrow it. Dyslexics do not outgrow the problem and must learn to cope with it.

3. Limited intelligence. Some children have intelligence that is lower than average. Though their learning capacity is reduced, the great majority of such children have the potential to master sufficient skills to lead happy, independent lives as adults.

4. Emotional problems or behavior disorders, sometimes resulting from the learning challenge itself, sometimes from other causes.

Seeking Professional Help

If you think there may be a serious problem, do not assume that it will go away. It is better to seek help, and the sooner the better.

Parents who have only one child may not readily understand that the child is slipping behind children of the same age. Even parents of several children may have difficulty in recognizing that a child is not performing up to expectations. Thus, while it is unfair to compare children with other children in certain respects, parents must not blind themselves to situations that arise in almost every family. The problem may be one that can readily be solved, or it may be one that requires much expert attention. In any case, nothing is gained by pretending it is not there. The delay that results from lack of attention may well cause the problem to grow worse with time. Get help.

If your child is not yet in school, discuss the problem with your physician. With school-age children, seek help from teachers and other school personnel. Most school systems have reading specialists, psychologists, speech and language therapists, counselors, and other professionals on staff.

ENGLISH AS A SECOND LANGUAGE

Millions of children in the United States primarily speak, read, and write a foreign language. For these children to succeed in our society, it is important that they learn to speak and read English. Two types of programs are available in schools.

Bilingual programs provide instruction in both English and the students' native language. Children are taught English; at the same time, they receive instruction in other subjects in their native language. When they are ready to handle subjects like math and science in English, they transfer to regular classes.

ESL, or English as a second language, programs function much like a foreign language course. They teach students how to read, write, and speak English. The use of native languages is not encouraged in class.

For information on these programs, contact The National Clearinghouse for Bilingual Education at 800-336-4560.

Children with Special Needs

There are many programs for children with special needs. There are remedial reading and remedial math programs. There are programs for the handicapped and for the gifted. All are based on the understanding that different children have different needs and abilities, and that all children deserve to be encouraged to learn to the best of their ability.

Some parents find it difficult to accept the fact that their children have learning problems. But it is important that parents do accept the situation, for that is a key step in helping children to cope with their problems. Also, it is important that parents do not indicate to their children that they are disappointed in them. If children feel rejected, they will probably not achieve their potential, and additional behavior problems may develop.

Make certain that the children have successful experiences in some areas of their lives. They may have difficulty in reading but be good at sports. Recognize and applaud their achievements. Use their interest in sports as a basis for reading. Find biographies of famous sports figures, encourage the following of reports of sports activities in the newspaper, and so on.

Through hard work and the support of parents and teachers, many children learn to overcome their learning difficulties. They may go on to have successful school and business careers. Thomas Edison, Winston Churchill, Albert Einstein, and Nelson Rockefeller all had learning problems early in school, yet they went on to make important contributions to society. Use such people as models for your children. Let the children know they are not alone.

HERE'S HELP

The following organizations can provide information on learning, vision, hearing, and other disabilities.

American Speech-Language-Hearing Association, 10801 Rockville Pike, Rockville, MD 20852. Publishes information on such topics as recognition of communication disorders.

Association for Children and Adults with Learning Disabilities, 4156 Library Road, Pittsburgh, PA 15234. Provides support and information concerning people with adequate intelligence who have learning disabilities.

Council for Exceptional Children, 1920 Association Drive, Reston, VA 22091. Provides information concerning children whose instructional needs differ sufficiently from the average to require special services.

National Information Center for Handicapped Children and Youth, P.O. Box 1492, Washington, D.C. 20003. Provides information to parents of children with physical, mental, and emotional handicaps.

Orton Dyslexia Society, 724 York Road, Baltimore, MD 21204. Offers publications dealing with the treatment of dyslexia and other language development problems.

Chapter Ten

USING TELEVISION WISELY

WE LIVE IN AN ELECTRONIC AGE. This chapter focuses on how parents can best use television and computers with their children. It also contains suggestions on the use of tape recorders.

HOW TELEVISION AFFECTS CHILDREN

Television plays a dominant role in many children's lives. It is common for children in elementary school to spend 5 hours a day watching television—almost as much time as they spend in school. Even if children spend considerably less time watching television, the time spent in this way is rarely quality time. Rather, it is time taken away from reading books, creating artwork, playing and talking with friends and parents, and other important activities. Numerous studies have examined the impact of television on children. In general, they have found that television viewing in the majority of American homes does more harm than good.

Many Negative Aspects

One of your main concerns is to help your children develop their full intellectual potential. Television viewing may interfere with this goal because it encourages passivity. Children are not asked to do anything but sit and watch. They are not asked to use their imaginations or even to think. In addition, children who watch a great deal of television usually do not spend enough time practicing reading, speaking, and other language skills.

Another important objective of parents for their children is character development. Children learn attitudes by watching people, including the characters on TV programs. Do these characters represent values you want for your children? Many TV characters are aggressive and violent, and of questionable morals.

Researchers have found that children who are exposed to television violence have an increased tendency to be aggressive. These children may have difficulties in school behavior, in large part because they come to believe that violence is an acceptable way to solve problems. Violence is used even in comic situations on television. Viewers are supposed to laugh when one cartoon character hits another on the head.

Positive Aspects

When used properly, television is a valuable tool. "Sesame Street" and other educational programs designed for children emphasize reading and counting skills as well as social skills such as cooperation. Nature programs introduce children to the lives of plants and animals. Travel programs introduce children to foreign lands and to cultures different from their own.

There is some evidence that television viewing enlarges the vocabulary of young children and helps them as they begin to learn to read. As children see the name of a product flashed on the screen and hear the announcer say the name, they learn sight-sound relationships. However, by the time children are nine or ten, television is reported to have a negative effect on language skills.

MAKING THE BEST OF IT

Some parents and many experts feel it is best not to allow any regular television viewing, but most families are not prepared to establish such a policy. Instead of attempting to abolish television, use it in ways that meet your values.

Establish Viewing Guidelines

The most important step is to set limits on what children may watch on television and how much time they may spend watching. Determine how much time your children spend watching television during a typical week. With this information, decide on reasonable time limits.

Next, decide what times during the day are not for TV viewing. Children normally should not be allowed to stay up past their bedtimes to watch television. Rest and sleep are more important than anything they may learn from most TV programs. They should never be allowed to watch television while doing their homework. This is a case in which two things cannot be done at once. And there should be no TV viewing during meals. It tends to encourage poor table manners and it interferes with the opportunity for family members to talk with one another.

Finally, make a list of acceptable programs for your children and a list of unacceptable programs. At a family conference explain why you are imposing viewing limits. Make it clear you are not doing so to punish your children but to enrich their lives. Let them know you understand the adjustment may be difficult, but you will help them find better ways to occupy their time. Generally, children accept rules on TV viewing if the rules are consistently enforced and if the children are given interesting alternatives.

Ask Questions

Build on your children's appropriate TV viewing by asking about a program they watched. What was the story? Where did it take place? Was the main character interesting? In what way? If the program was about nature or people of distant lands, ask what was the most exciting thing they learned or how their lives compare with the lives portrayed on the program. After seeing a television program with your children, discuss it with them. Do the characters on the program really exist? In what ways are they real? In what ways are they pretend? Are the characters intended to be role models of appropriate behavior?

Commercials also provide an opportunity to strengthen thinking skills. Children who are heavy TV viewers see 20,000 commercials a year. Even those whose TV viewing is limited are exposed to dozens of commercials every week. Without your help, children may be unable to evaluate claims they hear. Ask them whether the characters in a commercial are real people in a real world, whether they are speaking naturally or saying words someone wrote.

Encourage Reading

Use your children's television interests to stimulate learning and creativity. Children will enjoy reading books related to their favorite TV shows. Books that have been adapted for television are particularly popular. If children have enjoyed a TV special on Pearl Harbor or Teddy Roosevelt or the Olympic Games, borrow a book on the subject from your library's children's section and read it together. Compare the book and the TV program.

Parents and children can find many meaningful yet enjoyable alternatives to watching television.

There's Nothing to Do

Weaning children from television is easiest if you offer entertaining alternatives. Here are a few suggestions:

1. Spend an evening making cookies for the children to take to school. Let the children cut out the cookies, then decorate them with raisins and icing.

2. Take a walk. Walking provides opportunities for talking. Go to a park where children can use swings, to a playing field where a ball game is in progress, to an orchard where you can pick your own fruit. Occasionally include a special treat: "I didn't make dessert for dinner, so after we wash the dishes we can walk downtown and buy ice cream cones."

3. Play a board game or assemble a jigsaw puzzle.

4. Have a new hobby or craft to share, such as making model airplanes or stencil paintings.

5. Organize games, walks, and other activities that include your children's friends. Their parents also may be concerned about too much television.

LOOK, MA! I'M A STAR!

If you have home video equipment with recording capability, put your children on television. Film them as they read, act out a story, recite a poem, or play a musical instrument. During playback, help the children analyze their performances. Retape the activity if they wish to try again.

COMPUTERS

By the time your children are adults, they will probably have to be able to use computers if they are to find interesting jobs. The U.S. Department of Labor estimates that 50 to 75 percent of the jobs in the next generation will be related to computers.

This does not mean your children have to become computer experts by the time they are six or seven. But some children as young as four can use, enjoy, and benefit from computers. So if you have a computer at home, show your children how it works and encourage them to use it for activities appropriate to their age and interests. Before you know it, the children will be comfortable with computers.

Older children are even more eager to use computers, to play games but also for educational purposes. Children enjoy educational programs because they like being able to move at their own pace rather than at the pace set by a teacher. And they do not feel embarrassed about making mistakes. The computer does not criticize them for incorrect answers.

Educational Software

Computer software, or programs, designed to teach educational skills fall roughly into three categories.

Tutorials: Programs that teach new knowledge. Tutorials are available for everything from basic arithmetic and spelling to college chemistry.

Drill and practice: Programs that emphasize repetitive practice. They are designed to reinforce previously taught concepts. For prereaders there are programs that drill letter, number, and color recognition. Other programs ask children to match shapes and to use directional concepts.

Vocabulary and arithmetic drills are available for all levels. There are music drills that help students learn to recognize musical notes and musical notation. Some of these even encourage children to write their own songs.

Many drills are designed as games. In a best-selling typing drill, the player must correctly type words in order to protect the planet against alien invaders. In another game, the player must match fractions in order to stay in the game.

Computers are an increasingly important part of our world. Many children, more "computer literate" than most adults, are teaching their parents how to use computers.

Simulations: Models of real or imaginary worlds. They set up such situations as flying an airplane or managing a railroad or operating a nuclear power plant. One such program takes players on a trip to the South Pole and requires them to determine how many sleds and dogs will be needed for the trip.

Other Programs to Consider

One of the primary uses of personal computers is in *word processing* for writing letters, reports, or other documents. Even young children seem to benefit from using word-processing software to learn to write. Older children enjoy writing on the computer because it is so easy to make changes. Push a button or two and you can change words, correct punctuation, or reorganize a paragraph. The computer eliminates the need to rewrite every word of a story to produce a final draft.

Somewhat similar to word-processing programs are programs that enable people to create newspapers and other publications. Some of these *desktop publishing* programs are designed specifically for children. These programs let children experiment creatively as they write newspapers, posters, and so on.

Do not overlook software designed strictly for entertainment. Such programs may help develop important skills. For example, many games require players to use problem-solving skills such as strategy planning and reasoning. Some help develop eye-hand coordination and an understanding of spatial relationships.

Choosing Software

Selecting software for your children involves many of the same decisions as in buying books. Here are some things to consider when evaluating a program:

1. Is it appropriate for your child's interests? If you have two children with different interests, do not buy something that appeals only to one of them and expect the other to want to use it.

2. Does the package identify the age group the program is designed for? Does it indicate the learning skills that are developed?

3. Is the program easy to use? Children should be able to use it with little help from parents. Be ready, however, to provide some help, at least at first. If you cannot preview the program before you buy it, read reviews in computer magazines. Teachers are another good source of recommendations.

4. Does the program have more than one skill level so it can

provide a continuing challenge as the children's abilities increase? If so, does the program enable children to choose the level of difficulty they want?

5. How good are the instructions that accompany the program? They should be clearly written. They should explain how the program works and what it is designed to accomplish.

TAPE RECORDERS

Tape recorders are popular among children. Although these machines are used primarily to play music, they have some educational uses. Most libraries have audio cassettes that can be borrowed. Look for cassettes of famous poets reading their work, of old-time radio programs, of readings of worthwhile books.

Make a recording of your children reading a story or a poem or telling a story of their own. Then play back the recording. Children will enjoy hearing themselves and will learn to speak more clearly. They will recognize ways that they can improve their speech. For example, many children pepper their speech with *er, ah, you know,* and other distracting, meaningless sounds. Listening to themselves on tape can help rid them of this habit.

Older children may use tape recorders to interview grandparents and other adult relatives for a family history. Instead of writing letters to grandparents, they may choose to send tapes. Each family member can speak into the microphone, sharing news with Grandma and Grandpa. Children may read a poem, sing a song, or play something on the piano.

Chapter Eleven

EXCURSIONS NEAR AND FAR

FROM BIRTH ONWARD the world of children expands, and sharing in the excitement is one of the rewards of parenthood. Few experiences surpass the joy of watching the expressions on children's faces when they first touch a puppy, go to a zoo, watch a parade, or take a boat ride.

Yet, introducing children to the world in which they live is more than mere pleasure. By familiarizing children with this world and making them comfortable about exploring it, parents help ensure that their children will be productive members of society.

A trip is usually successful if it is planned and discussed with children ahead of time. Talk with them about where you will be going and what they will see and do. This is particularly important if you are going somewhere quite different from places the children already have visited.

Borrow related books from the library. If you are going to visit the home of a famous poet, for example, read some poems by that poet before you go, as well as after you return. If you plan a trip to an aquarium, books on sharks and dolphins will heighten children's enthusiasm. If the trip will be a long one, show children a map of where you will be going. Tell them how long the trip will take and what they may see on the way.

If your children are old enough, let them help in the preparations. Before a trip to a distant place, have the children write to tourist bureaus for brochures. If you are going on a picnic, have the children help prepare potato salad or brownies. On the day of the picnic, have them count out plates and eating utensils.

Make certain the children are appropriately dressed for the trip. Are they wearing proper shoes for ground and weather conditions and for the amount of walking you plan to do? Do they have jackets or sweaters for late in the day, when temperatures are expected to drop? Are they taking more equipment and other belongings than can be comfortably carried? Carrying too much is tiring and can limit your activities.

KEEP CHILDREN OCCUPIED

On long trips children tend to get restless.

1. Take along a box of paper, crayons, and other items for the children to use.

2. Play I Spy. Take turns choosing something that everyone is to look for—a bookstore, a black dog, a person wearing a striped jacket. The first person to find it says, "I spy!" A variation of this game begins with one person saying, "I spy something that rhymes with *night*" or "I spy something that flies." The other people then try to find the object.

3. Keep a list of the animals shown on billboards along the way.

4. Have the children draw all the traffic signs you pass. Underneath each picture they can write words explaining what the sign means.

5. Ask children to follow the trip's progress on a map. Ask them how far you have traveled, and how many miles remain until you reach your destination. Encourage them to watch for and read mileage and directional signs.

6. Encourage the children to take naps, particularly near the end of the trip, so they will be fresh for the adventure that lies ahead.

UPON ARRIVAL

It is not good to insist on a rigid schedule. If children want to spend 10 minutes watching sharks, do not try to pull them away to see seals. If a tiny flower growing from the crack in a sidewalk draws their attention, look at it with them.

Remember that young children have limited attention spans. Take breaks to rest or have something to eat. If you are visiting a museum or historic building, leave the building for a while and go in again after your children have had a chance to run around.

Have an interesting tidbit to share with the children. This might be a fascinating fact related to what the children are viewing, or a riddle or joke.

BUILD ON EXCURSIONS

Trips become more meaningful, and memories of them more lasting, if you expand on them once you are back home. Here are some suggestions.

1. Talk about the experience. What did the children like best? Why? What was most unexpected? Would they like to visit the place again?

2. Encourage your children to tell others about the trip and write about what they saw, heard, and did.

3. Make a scrapbook of things collected during the trip: postcards, used ticket stubs, maps of the travel route, menus, brochures, etc. Ask your children to write captions for the items or to tell you what the captions should say. If the children make drawings of what they have seen, include them in the scrapbook.

4. If you make slides or movies, plan a family show during which everyone can relive the trip.

5. Borrow library books: a biography of a famous person whose home you visited, a collection of poems about the sea, a story about pioneer life.

6. Share a craft that relates to the trip. After a winter walk, show the children how to make snowflakes from paper. Use them to decorate a window or Christmas tree. After visiting an Indian reservation, make beaded necklaces or model tepees.

7. Encourage imaginative play based on the experience, for example, pretending to be an airplane pilot, or preparing a doll for a visit to a hospital.

8. Watch for and share relevant articles in newspapers and magazines: an article describing the parade you attended, an article about plants like those you saw, an article about a concert you attended.

LOTS OF PLACES TO VISIT

An excursion can take an hour or two, half a day, several days. It can be merely a walk through a park during a trip to the supermarket or a journey to a distant city. Most young children are interested in animals, so zoos are always popular. A child who eagerly studies the violin may enjoy going to a concert featuring a violinist. Plan trips so children can use skills they have learned. Eating in a restaurant lets children show they have learned proper table manners. Putting out a fire safely at a campground lets them practice safety.

Your Community

Gradually familiarize young children with places in your community. At the post office let children put mail in the slots, watch packages being weighed, see the different kinds of stamps. Explain that you must pay to send letters and packages, and that the heavier something is, the more it costs to send. Explain that stamps are like money, and that each kind of stamp has a specific value.

Watch people at work—trimming trees, painting a building, setting up a store window display. Show that asking questions is part of learning about the things you see. For instance, at a building site, watch the progress from week to week.

Ask questions of your children to help strengthen their observation skills. At the construction site, ask them what the machines are doing and how the workers are dressed. At an airport, ask where people get on planes, how the plane gets fuel, where the passengers sit, how the luggage gets onto the plane.

Some businesses may sponsor tours or open houses. Watch newspapers for announcements of special events, such as parades, fireworks displays, and outdoor concerts.

Take walks at night. Things look different in the dark. Lights come from house windows, there are stars in the sky, and so on. Things also sound and smell different. Encourage children to use their senses. Why do you think the dog is barking? Is someone burning wood or cooking hamburgers on an outdoor grill? Is there a skunk in the neighborhood?

An excursion to a railroad crossing provides an opportunity to tell young children about trains, their safety, their components, and how they operate.

Parks are ideal environments in which to learn about birds, squirrels, and other creatures.

During Walks

Play the game of Same and Different. How are those two cars the same? How are they different? Play a counting game. How many cars are parked on this street? How many signs are in that store window? How many cows are in the field?

Find out how things feel. Use terms such as *rough, smooth, bumpy, soft, hard, sharp, cold, warm, wet, dry, same, different.* If children do not know some of these terms, introduce them. For instance, as they touch a tree, say, "The bark of this tree feels rough. Find something else that feels rough." Then ask the children to find something that feels smooth.

Parks and Nature Preserves

These are great places to study nature and to develop large-muscle skills: running, jumping, climbing, throwing. Take along a field guide so you and your children can identify plants and animals you see. Binoculars will make it easier to watch birds. A compass can be used to teach directions. Find out what activities are available. If there are park rangers, they may lead walks, show films, or demonstrate crafts.

Help your children develop a feeling of responsibility for the environment. Do not let them litter. Do not let them remove plants from roadsides or along pathways. If there are designated trails, instruct the children to stay on them. Explain to your children what would happen to the habitat if everyone visiting the park or nature

77

preserve dug up plants or walked through nesting areas or left litter on the ground or in ponds.

Zoos

Most zoos are too large to be covered in a single visit. Select certain animals to observe on each visit. Some zoos are designed especially for young children. Such a zoo can be seen in a single visit, but most children will want repeat trips to feed the ducks and pet the sheep again.

Museums

There are all sorts of museums: toy, doll, natural history, art, science, history, costume, sports, even children's museums. All are fascinating, showing us things we might otherwise be unable to see. Many museums have special programs for children, such as films and art appreciation classes.

Children are most interested in three-dimensional objects, such as masks, mummies, puppets, armor, and dinosaur skeletons. They relate well to things they can touch, which makes science museums excellent places to visit. They especially like places they can walk into, such as historic houses and reconstructed Indian villages.

When you visit an art museum, try to find things children like: paintings of birds or pets, paintings of children in clothing worn long ago, and paintings of action scenes.

After visiting a museum, discuss why people collect things: to study and learn; because they are pretty, valuable, have family meaning. Encourage your children to start collections of their own.

LEARNING ABOUT SAFETY

Trips provide excellent opportunities to introduce children to important safety habits: the need to obey traffic rules, the proper way to cross streets, how to recognize poisonous plants, why people should not take glass to a beach, and so on.

Chapter Twelve

DEVELOPING LIBRARY SKILLS

HELP YOUR CHILDREN LEARN library skills by first learning them yourself. Ask the librarian for a booklet that describes what the library contains and where things are located. Ask if someone can give you a library tour. The more you know about the library, the better you can help your children. Ask if there are special activities and exhibits intended for children. Most of all, browse. Browsing will lead you to interesting things to read for your own sake and your children's.

To remove a library book from the shelf, hold the book in the middle of the spine. This prevents damage to the book's cover.

INTRODUCING THE LIBRARY

If you make going to the library a habit, you will be taking your children there while they are still quite young, just as you will take them to the supermarket and other local places. They will accept the library as a part of their world long before they learn its purpose and appreciate its value.

By the time they are toddlers, children will show an interest in the book-selection process. Begin introducing them to the children's section. Tell them that all the books in this section were written especially for children. Point out that the books can be read in the library or taken home. Explain that to take a book home, it must be checked out at a special desk, and that you need a library card in order to check it out. Let the children see that the librarian makes a record of the books you borrow. Show the children the date stamped in the books, and explain that this tells you how long you may keep the book. Take excursions centered around returning the book, and borrow some more. Reinforce the idea that the library is a part of your family life.

Build children's familiarity with the library over a series of visits. For instance, you might ask the children if they want to borrow fairy tales or books about animals. Once they make a choice, ask them if they know where that type of book is found.

Even at this early age, stress the fact that people behave well in the library, and that the books and other library materials are to be treated carefully. Teach your children to turn the pages of a book gently, so they do not tear them.

Story hours and other activities for young children provide opportunities for your children to be with other children and to practice proper group behavior. These occasions reinforce the idea of a library as an enjoyable place. Many storytellers have a flair for drama. They know how to make stories come to life.

YOUNG READERS

Once children begin to read, they will find books on their own, though you should make occasional suggestions.

How Books Are Arranged

Point out the signs on the book stacks. These may indicate the kinds of books found in the stacks—fiction, history, science, etc.— or they may give a range of numbers or letters. Explain that the numbers and letters are part of the system used by the library to store books.

Most community libraries in the United States use the Dewey Decimal System to catalog nonfiction books. This system assigns specific class numbers to books. All the books on a certain subject have the same class number. They are placed together on the library shelves and are arranged alphabetically by the first letter of the author's last name.

Other Areas of the Library

Once youngsters become familiar with the layout of the children's section, you may begin introducing them to other areas. Point out that the adult section is arranged much like the children's section. Spend time with them in the periodicals section, where you and your children can read magazines. If the library has records, art prints, or videotapes that circulate, show these to your children. Together, choose some to borrow and enjoy at home.

On Their Own

Encourage your children to browse. Show them how reading titles of books on a shelf can lead to interesting finds. Browsing requires time, so plan to spend an hour or more at the library. You might indicate to the children that you want to read a particular magazine, or that you need some time to do research for a letter you are writing to the local newspaper editor. Tell them they can spend the time in browsing, find a magazine to read, or look at a special exhibit. Expect them to do something productive. Do not let them sit by your side doing nothing.

Encourage your children to ask librarians for help when they cannot find what they want. Librarians are willing to aid children in their search for information and to help them acquire basic library skills.

OLDER, INDEPENDENT CHILDREN

Once children become independent readers, they will begin to express interest in the adult section of the library. Even before this time, however, you can make them aware that there are books in the adult section that will appeal to them. Take out illustrated books on animals, hobbies, or airplanes and spend time at home going through the books together. Take out books of folk songs and have the entire family learn a song or two. Take out cookbooks and have your children help choose a recipe.

Periodicals

Children's periodicals usually are kept in the children's section, but there will be many periodicals in the adult section that will interest your children, particularly magazines such as *National Wildlife* and those covering popular music and sports. Find out if issues may be borrowed. If not, encourage your children to take the time to read magazines in the library.

AN IMPORTANT MILESTONE

How old must children be to become eligible for library cards? Check with the librarian. When your children reach this age, help them apply for cards. Let the children know that getting a library card is a sign that they are growing up, and that it demonstrates your confidence that they appreciate the responsibilities involved in using a library.

REFERENCE MATERIALS

Most libraries have reference sections filled with nonfiction books useful for school subjects. Show your children the many types of books found in a reference section.

Encyclopedias. An encyclopedia is an excellent place to begin researching a subject. Some encyclopedias cover the entire range of knowledge. Others focus on specific topics, such as animals or movies. Some are designed especially for children, while others are more suitable for advanced readers.

Dictionaries. Children will be fascinated by the many kinds of dictionaries available, ranging from the giant unabridged versions to dictionaries on specific topics.

Atlases and gazetteers. An atlas is a collection of maps. The maps may be of towns, states, countries, even stellar constellations. A gazetteer is a geographical dictionary. It lists places alphabetically, tells where they are, and gives other information about them.

Almanacs. An almanac is an annual publication filled with statistical and other factual information, such as population figures, election results, Nobel Prize winners, major earthquakes, baseball batting averages, and tide tables.

Suggested Activities

Point out that people use all sorts of references to find information. Name some common reference materials in your home: address book, telephone book, street map, dictionary, cookbook, first aid manual. Can your children add to the list?

Family conversations often include questions or disputes on factual material: What is the distance from New York to Paris? Where was Franklin D. Roosevelt born? What is the difference between a crocodile and an alligator? If your home library does not supply the answers to such questions, you may wish to purchase an encyclopedia or other reference book.

WHAT'S IN A BOOK?

Children can best use a book if they understand its structure. As children begin to read, show them the various parts of books and explain the purposes of each.

Front matter. The pages before the text of a book are its front matter. These pages include a *title page,* which gives the book's full title and the name of the author or, in some cases, the editor. Usually, there also is a *table of contents.* It lists the chapters or other divisions of the book, and gives the page number on which each division begins.

The body, or text. This is the main part of the book.

Bibliography. The bibliography is a list of books and articles. It may be a list of the publications used by the author in writing the book or it may be a list of recommended publications on the subject. Each entry in the bibliography includes the title of the book or article, the author or editor, the publisher, and the date of publication. The bibliography usually is found at the end of the text. Some books have a bibliography at the end of each chapter. In encyclopedias, there may be a bibliography at the end of each article.

Glossary. A glossary is a list of words used in the book with their definitions.

Index. Most nonfiction books contain an index, an alphabetical guide to information in the book. The index indicates the topics presented in the book and the pages on which each topic is discussed. The index is at the back of a book.

THE DEWEY DECIMAL SYSTEM

Below are the ten main classes of the Dewey Decimal System. Each class is subdivided. For instance, a book on the history of Africa has the class number 960, while one on the history of North America has 970. One on the history of the Pacific Coast states has 979, while one that only covers the history of Oregon has 979.5.

    000 GENERAL WORKS
    100 PHILOSOPHY AND PSYCHOLOGY
    200 RELIGION
    300 SOCIAL SCIENCES
    400 SCIENCE
    500 NATURAL SCIENCE
    600 APPLIED SCIENCE AND USEFUL ARTS
    700 FINE ARTS AND RECREATION
    800 LITERATURE
    900 HISTORY, GEOGRAPHY, BIOGRAPHY

Chapter Thirteen

DEVELOPING STUDY HABITS

KNOWING HOW TO STUDY AND LEARN is helpful throughout life. The same habits needed to do school work are needed by adults learning new skills, reading and writing reports, preparing for meetings, and so on. You can foster good study habits in your children by establishing routines at home. Numerous studies have shown that structure is important for children. They feel more secure and succeed better in school if they live in an environment that is consistent and predictable.

To have a structured environment, there should be regular places in which to eat, sleep, and study. There also should be set times to eat, sleep, and study. Remember, your goal is not a rigid structure but one with a sense of organization. Children begin to learn organization shortly after birth, when a routine is established for feeding and bathing and napping. Once children are toddlers, they can begin to learn the value of organizing their toys, clothes, and other belongings. The responsibility for maintaining their belongings should gradually pass from you to them.

Help your child discover that dictionaries are valuable reference tools not only for homework but also for leisure reading, crossword puzzles, and other activities.

ESTABLISH A STUDY ROUTINE

Once a child reaches school age, the schedule should include a time for doing homework. If possible, schedule study time at the same time each day. Even the best plans are easily sabotaged if you allow it. In some cases, you can head off trouble. For example, place the telephone off limits during study time, and have the children tell their friends not to call during that time. On all matters, firmness is the key. Make it clear that work comes before play.

The amount of time that should be devoted to studying depends on the children's ages, the subjects they are learning, and how well they are doing in school. It is a good idea to ask teachers at the beginning of the school year how much time will be needed. Check again during the year if your children are having problems. If your children say they have no homework at all, be sure to ask their teachers.

Decide with your children when they will study. Some children prefer to study right after school. Others prefer to study after supper. What should not be allowed is a time late at night, when children are not fully alert.

HOMEWORK: A FACT OF LIFE

Research shows that well-planned homework increases learning. Many children see homework as drudgery, punishment, or an unpleasant chore. It is important that parents try to prevent the development of such attitudes. Let your children know you think of homework as an opportunity to build knowledge.

Homework is a responsibility that children must learn to accept, just as they will someday have to accept the responsibilities involved in having a job. Teachers expect homework to be done neatly, correctly, and on time. If the homework does not meet standards, it is the children's responsibility, not yours. You are there to guide them, but it is not your job to know what the homework is or when it is due. Do not let children pressure you into helping to build a science project that is due the next day but only begun the night before, despite the fact that the project was assigned two weeks ago. By giving in to such pleas, you encourage children to shirk responsibility.

Write It Down

It is easy to forget an assignment or become confused about which problems are to be completed and when. Point out to your children that everyone has difficulty remembering such things. That is why you make shopping lists and write down appointments. Give your children notebooks in which to write down their assignments.

It is also good for children to keep schedules of their after-school activities. This helps them organize time efficiently. Begin by introducing young children to daily schedules. You might help them make up the next day's schedule, perhaps just before supper. Post schedules for each of your children in a place where the schedules can be seen easily, perhaps on a bulletin board in the kitchen.

Parents can explain directions, check answers, and in other ways help with homework, but children should do the actual work themselves.

When Should You Help?

Let your children know you are always available to help, but they must do the homework themselves. You can review arithmetic with them or discuss the meaning of words or explain directions, but you must not do the assignments. If you provide the answers, build the project, or do the research for a report, you are defeating the purpose of homework.

It is a good idea to establish a routine of looking at completed assignments, particularly with children who are just learning about homework. Check for the following:

- Did the child follow directions?
- Is all the work done? If not, why? Perhaps the child did not understand what was to be done.
- Is the work neat?
- Are the answers correct?

Praise children for work well done. Provide guidance if the work is not correct. Also discuss the assignments with your children. Was the homework difficult? Interesting? Did it help them understand material taught in school?

As it becomes apparent that children recognize the responsibilities involved in doing homework, feel comfortable about talking with you about difficulties they encounter, and consistently do neat, relatively error-free work, you need not check homework each day. However, your children may prefer that you do. If you make the process enjoyable, your children will appreciate your interest and look forward to the opportunity to discuss their accomplishments with you.

A Place to Study

Setting up a study area shows that you recognize the importance of your children's work. The area should include a table or desk with a drawer or other container for pencils, rulers, and other basic tools. It should have a comfortable, child-sized chair and the light should be good. There should be a bookcase or shelf for the child's personal library, or at least a spot for a dictionary or any other reference books the child needs.

The study area should be quiet, with few if any distractions. Children should not be allowed to watch television during their study time. Regardless of what they would like to believe, people cannot study when a TV set is on.

Parents also must respect their children's need for quiet during study time. If you are watching television in another room, keep the sound down. Many students work well when a radio is set to supply soft music. If your children say they work better when they have music playing, permit them to have a radio on.

A GOOD DICTIONARY

One of the best gifts for children is a dictionary. There are several quality dictionaries designed especially for children. Some are geared toward young children with limited reading skills. Others are more suitable for intermediate readers.

After you present the dictionary, spend some time with the children to help them discover what it contains. Be sure to point out these essential features:

1. Correct spelling of words.
2. Proper place to break a word into syllables.
3. Correct way to pronounce words.
4. Meanings of words and examples of how to use them.
5. Proper grammatical forms of words.

Point out that the defined words are listed in alphabetical order and ask your children to find some words. For example, which comes first, *bake* or *cake? Pan* or *pen? By* or *buy? Grandmother* or *grandfather? Zoo* or *zone?*

Usually, there are *guide words* at the top of each page. They indicate the first and last words on the page and make it easy to locate words in the dictionary.

Help your children find some *homographs.* These are words that are spelled the same but have different meanings and different pronunciations. For example, a "bass" is a type of fish—and the lowest male singing voice. "Wind" is a current of air—and a verb meaning to wrap something around another object. "Bow" is a weapon used with an arrow—and a verb meaning to bend at the waist.

Often, there are special features in the back of the dictionary, such as a list of biographical entries or a list of geographic places. Point out that these are like mini-dictionaries. Items within each list are in alphabetical order. (Next time you and your children go to the library, look at the large biographical and geographical dictionaries in the reference section.)

As your children get older, purchase more advanced dictionaries. These will contain more words than beginning dictionaries yet still be easier to read than adult editions. By high school, many children are ready to use adult dictionaries.

WHAT IS MEANT BY GOOD LIGHTING?

Good artificial lighting for a student means general room illumination plus an individual lamp with a 100-watt bulb. The bulb should be shaded so that the light does not shine into the reader's eyes.

Reading in the light of a lamp alone will cause unwanted reflections from the page; this can cause eye fatigue. Having an overhead light in addition to a lamp reduces the chance of glare.

If possible, avoid using fluorescent lamps for overhead lighting and never use fluorescent lamps for individual lighting. The faint, but noticeable, flicker of fluorescent lamps also can contribute to fatigue.

The lamp should be placed at a student's left side if the student is right-handed, at the right side if the student is left-handed. This prevents undesirable shadows across the page.

Chapter Fourteen

YOU AND MY FUN
WITH LEARNING

MY FUN WITH LEARNING is designed for families with children between 18 months and 12 years. This does not mean 18-month-old children will read the set. They will benefit from sitting in your lap and pointing out objects with which they are familiar as well as learning the names of new objects. It is never too early to expose children to the joys of books. Older preschoolers will enjoy turning pages and hearing you read stories. Grade school children will profit from reading an exciting variety of topics, from simple stories to selections that open up the worlds of science, nature, history, and mathematics.

Children prefer materials that are heavily and attractively illustrated in short, self-contained articles. They also prefer selections that are clearly and excitingly written and that combine education and entertainment. *My Fun with Learning* was designed with these preferences in mind.

As a parent, you have taken a great stride forward with your children in adding this set of books to your home library. It provides a means for you to involve your children in the process of learning in an enjoyable way. In the time you spend reading aloud from the volumes, in the time your children spend reading to you and later to themselves, a great deal will occur that will be positive both for you and for your children.

You will gain a deeper understanding of your children, in regard to their day-by-day development as well as their potential. Your children will begin to acquire a lifelong respect for and attachment to the world of books. This last is a priceless achievement. But there is an even greater benefit. By using *My Fun with Learning* with your children, you will make even stronger the natural bond between parent and child that forms the basis for the highest mutual respect and love that families can achieve. Thus, the joint activities that await you in these volumes will benefit you and your family many times over in the years that lie ahead. The success in life that you wish for your children will be more readily achievable as a direct outcome of the shared hours of reading and discovery.

There are many ways to use *My Fun with Learning* with your children as well as many ways in which they will enjoy using the books on their own.

Reading Stories

Children may read the stories in sequence, beginning with the first story in a volume, gradually reading all the way through the book. But it is much more likely that children will dip into one volume, then another, to find a story that interests them at a particular moment.

Use these books to expand on activities in your children's daily lives. If your children enjoy animals, suggest they read "The Animal Kingdom" in Book Three. If they are learning to play baseball, read "Baseball" in Book Two, which defines baseball terms and explains the rules of the game. By glancing through the table of contents in each book, you will be sure to find many topics to recommend to your children.

Children's interests are constantly changing and expanding.

Many of the stories in these books will fascinate children who are very young. Other stories may not interest the youngest children but will attract them when they are a year or two older.

Many parts of these books will appeal to children year after year, for each time they read a particular part they may discover something previously overlooked. Some sections will delight pre-schoolers but may bore their older brothers and sisters, who would much prefer reading the material geared to older children.

Reading a story from one of the volumes is a pleasant way to spend part of an evening or a rainy afternoon. There are many ways to introduce this:

"You were asking about the moon the other day. Let's read this article."

"Grandma sent us a postcard from the place where the first plane was flown. Here's a good story about the two brothers who built and flew that plane."

If children show special interest in a story, try to carry the interest further. The next time you and the children go to the library, look for books on the subject. Plan a trip to a museum that has exhibits related to the subject.

Looking Things Up

Use these books to help your children learn how to find information. Show them how to use the index in this book, then encourage them to use this index to find answers to questions you ask and to questions they themselves ask.

"Where were the first Olympic Games held?"

"What is our state's nickname?"

"How big is your heart?"

The index is a guide to information in all books of *My Fun with Learning.* It tells where in the books a particular subject is discussed. Each index entry is followed by two numbers, for example, Eardrums 3:117. The first number indicates the book in which the subject is discussed. The second number is the page in that book where the information can be found. Sometimes a subject is covered on more than one page: Telegraph, invention of 4:148–149.

Some entries are followed by additional references, called subentries. These refer to aspects of the major entry. Finally, some entries end with "see also" and are followed by the name of another index entry. Such a listing tells the reader where to look for more information on the subject.

Doing Homework Assignments

Although *My Fun with Learning* is designed primarily for leisure reading, it also can be used by children in conjunction with their school work. If children are asked to prepare brief speeches for a class, they can get ideas and information for their speeches. If they need to write a report on a specific topic, such as the United Nations or life in the Old West, have them check the index at the end of this book to learn if the set contains information they can use.

BOOK ONE

Great Stories from World Literature. Here are poems as well as stories you loved as a child, that your children will love, and their children will love. Read these poems and stories to very young children. Later, let them read by themselves or aloud to younger brothers and sisters. If a story appeals to them especially, look in your library for more stories by the same author.

BOOK TWO

Book Two is in three sections.

The Earth and the Stars. Geology and astronomy come to life in this section, which contains articles on Earth, the solar system, and outer space. Chapters on the seven continents provide a lively and colorful introduction to geography. Young readers are fascinated by chapters such as "Weather," "Earth and Space," "The Planets," and "Rockets and Space Travel."

Adventures in Science and Discovery. This section covers a broad range of intriguing subjects. Children learn about early ways of counting and about the contributions of Pythagoras, Archimedes, Galileo, Newton, and many others to mathematics and science. They read about subjects ranging from ancient alchemy to modern rocketry. Here, too, are chapters on photography, radio, computers, lasers, and medicine.

The section's concluding chapter discusses ways young people can become involved in and learn more about science and describes some of today's most exciting new scientific fields.

Fact Book. This section is excellent for asking and answering questions. Children will browse through it on their own, for it contains all sorts of information that appeals to young and adult minds, including:

The largest, longest, tallest, and greatest wonders on earth.
A list of important events in human history.
Names and addresses of organizations for young people.
Weights and measurements.
Facts on U.S. Presidents, the 50 states, and U.S. government.
Rules for baseball, football, basketball, and soccer.
Rules for household, sports, traffic, and personal safety.

BOOK THREE

Plants and Animals. Living things fascinate children. This section introduces children to major types of plants and animals, with a special emphasis on the habitats in which they live. Use these articles to build on family excursions to zoos and parks. Then encourage your children further by borrowing library books that focus on specific creatures and how they live. Or help them create and maintain an aquarium.

All About You. This section introduces children to facts about the parts of the body and how they work. The section also contains articles on health and personal grooming. As in other sections of *My Fun with Learning,* words that are difficult or important are italicized and defined in simple terms. You and your growing children will find many occasions over the years to refer to articles in this section.

BOOK FOUR

Real-Life Heroes. This section presents the stories of 25 people who achieved outstanding success in life. Each story highlights the quality of character that helped each of these men and women realize their lifetime goals.

America's Story. This section covers the history of the United States, from the beginning to the modern age. Each chapter tells an interesting story and also provides young readers with valuable learning material. Some of the stories highlight important events in history, such as the writing of the Declaration of Independence and the entry of the United States into World War II. Other stories focus on individuals who made contributions to our civilization, such as Eli Whitney, Samuel F. B. Morse, and Charles Lindbergh.

When reading from Book Four, have a map or globe nearby. Refer to it when places are mentioned: Where is Philadelphia? Which state is it in? What other large cities are nearby?

RECOMMENDED READING

The following bibliography lists some of the best books currently available for parents who wish to encourage their children. For additional suggestions, ask your children's teachers and school and public librarians.

Coping with Kids and School by Linda Albert. E.P. Dutton, New York, 1984.

Getting Ready to Read by Betty D. Boegehold. Ballantine Books, New York, 1984.

Growing up Writing by Linda Leonard Lamme. Acropolis Books, Washington, D.C., 1984.

How Children Learn by John Holt. Dell Publishing, New York, 1983.

How to Raise a Brighter Child by Joan Beck. Putnam, New York, 1982.

Nature with Children of All Ages by Edith A. Sisson. Prentice-Hall, Englewood Cliffs, N.J., 1982.

Only the Best: The Discriminating Software Guide for Preschool-Grade 12 by Linda L. Mattas and the editors of SchoolTech News. Education News Service, Carmichael, Calif., 1986.

Schoolwise: A Parent's Guide to Getting the Best Education for Your Child by Martha C. Brown. Jeremy P. Tarcher, Los Angeles, 1985.

Teaching Television: How to Use TV to Your Child's Advantage by Dorothy G. Singer, Jerome L. Singer, and Diana M. Zuckerman. The Dial Press, New York, 1981.

The Mother's Almanac by Marguerite Kelly and Elia Parsons. Doubleday, New York, 1975.

The Read-Aloud Handbook by Jim Trelease. Penguin Books, New York, 1985.

The Toy Chest by Stevanne Auerbach. Lyle Stuart, New York, 1986.

What Did You Learn in School Today? by Bruce Baron, Christine Baron, and Bonnie MacDonald. Warner Communications, New York, 1983.

Your Child Is Smarter Than You Think by Peggy Eastman. William Morrow, New York, 1985.

Index

Index

L

M

Mercury (planet), 2:73, 2:76
Mercury (space program), 4:123
Mesopotamia, 2:99, 2:105
Metamorphic rock, 2:53
Meteor, 2:79
Meteorite, 2:79
Meteorology. *See* Weather
Methane, 2:78
Metric system, 2:229–232, 5:49
Mexico, 2:30, 2:205, 2:206, 2:208, 2:214, 4:150–153
Mexico City (Mex.), 2:208, 2:215
Michelangelo, 2:207
Michigan, 2:240, 2:244–245
Microbiology, 2:134
Microscope, 2:131–134, 2:150, 2:152, 2:178
Middle Ages, 2:27, 2:205
Middle East, 2:19
  history, 2:202–206, 2:209–210
Migration, of animals, 3:62–65
Miletus, 2:105
Milky Way galaxy, 2:80–82, 2:88–89, 2:188
Milne, A. A., 1:41
Milton, John, 2:208
Mind, 3:217
Minerals, 2:33, 2:41, 3:200, 3:203
Ming dynasty, 2:206, 2:208
Minicomputer, 2:175
Minnesota, 2:240, 2:244–245
Minoan civilization, 2:202, 2:203
Minuit, Peter, 4:113
Minutemen, 4:123–126
Mir spacecraft, 2:93, 2:222
Mississippi, 2:240, 2:244–245
Mississippi River, 2:8, 2:31, 2:199, 4:145–146, 4:148
Missouri, 2:240, 2:246–247
Missouri River, 2:199
Mitchell, Maria, 4:22–25
Mohammed. *See* Muhammad
Molars, 3:152
Molds, 2:166–167, 3:12

Molecule, 2:141, 2:145, 2:178
Mollusk, 3:20
Monaco, area of, 2:197
Monarch butterflies, 3:63
Money, 2:233–234, 5:50–51
Mongolia, 2:17
Mongols, 2:205, 2:206
Monkeys, 3:77
Monroe, James, 2:242
Montana, 2:246–247
Montcalm, Louis, 4:118
Montgomery (Ala.), 4:89–91
Moon, 2:68–71, 2:125
  base on, 2:93
  centrifugal force, 2:128
  distance, 2:69
  eclipse, 2:71
  far side, 2:69, 2:70
  gravity, 2:70, 2:71, 2:93, 2:128
  landing, 2:68, 2:214
  myths about, 2:68
  as natural satellite, 2:5, 2:69
  rocks, 2:5, 2:71, 2:91
  rotation, 2:69
  temperature, 2:70
Morocco, 2:210
Morphine, 3:191
Morse, Samuel, 4:155–157
Morse Code, 4:34, 4:155–157
Moscow (U.S.S.R.), 2:215
Moslems. *See* Islam
Moss, 2:22, 3:12, 3:14
Moth, 3:52–53
Mother Teresa, 2:226, 4:93–96
Motion, laws of, 2:129–130
Motor nerves, 3:158
Motors, electric, 2:147, 2:148
Mount Aconcagua, 2:33
Mountains, 2:8, 2:9, 2:56–57
  fault block, 2:46
  highest, 2:198
  weathering, 2:52
Mount Erebus, 2:21
Mount Everest, 2:19, 2:198

Mount Kilimanjaro, 2:37, 2:41
Mount Kosciusko, 2:41
Mount McKinley, 2:29, 2:198
Mouth, 3:152, 3:169, 3:173
Movie camera, 2:160
Mozart, Wolfgang Amadeus, 2:208
Mucous membrane, 3:147
Mucus, 3:171, 3:179
Muhammad, 2:205
Mule deer, 3:63
Mumps, 3:176
Muscles, 3:122, 3:131, 3:132,
    3:135–138
  cells, 3:126–127
  exercising, 3:164–169
  heart, 3:143–144
  involuntary, 3:136–138, 3:160
  voluntary, 3:136, 3:137, 3:160
Museums, 5:78
Music, 2:104, 2:109, 5:58
Musket, 4:144
Muslims. *See* Islam
Mussolini, Benito, 2:212, 4:197
Mysteries of Nature, The, 2:133
Myths, 2:25

N

Napoleon Bonaparte, 2:212, 4:146,
    4:147
Narcotics, 3:191
NATO, 2:212
Nature preserves, 5:77–78
Nauru, 2:197
Nazi Party, 4:197, 4:198, 4:200
Neap tide, 2:71
Nebraska, 2:246–247
Nebula, 2:82
Nectar, 3:45
Negative, 2:159
Neptune, 2:78
Nero, 2:205
Nerve cell, 3:126

Nerve ending, 3:168–169
Nerves, 3:156–160
  See also specific nerves
Nervous system, 3:160
Neuron, 3:156
Neutron, 2:143
Neutron star, 2:83
Nevada, 2:240, 2:246–247
New Amsterdam, 4:113–114
Newcomen, Thomas, 2:136
New Deal, 4:195–196
New Frontier, 4:209
New Guinea, 2:43, 2:197
New Hampshire, 2:239–240,
    2:246–247
New Jersey, 2:239–240,
    2:246–247
New Mexico, 2:246–247
New Netherland, 4:113, 4:114
New Orleans (La.), 4:145–146
Newton, Sir Isaac, 2:62, 2:72–73,
    2:126–130, 2:208, 4:48
New World, 2:27, 2:29, 2:30
New York City, 2:215, 2:239
New York State, 2:239–240,
    2:246–247
New York Stock Exchange, 4:193
New Zealand, 2:43
Nicaragua, 2:213
Niche, 10
Nickel, 2:8
Nicotine, 3:194
Niepce, Joseph, 2:156
Nigeria, 2:210
Nile River, 2:8, 2:34, 2:37–38, 2:99,
    2:199, 2:202
Nineveh, 2:203
Nitrogen, 2:54
Nitrogen base, 2:178, 2:179
Nixon, Richard M., 2:214, 2:243
Nobel Peace Prize winners,
    2:224–226
Normans, 2:206
North Africa, 2:205, 2:206

Sete Quedas (waterfall), 2:199
Seven Wonders of the World,
    2:219
Sex, 3:186
Shadow, 2:105
Shah of Iran, 2:209
Shakespeare, William, 2:207
Shale, 2:53
Shang dynasty, 2:202
Shanghai (China), 2:215
Shapes, 2:100, 2:106–107
Shepard, Alan B., Jr., 4:213
Shore, 3:90–93
Siberia, 2:19
Sierra Madre Mountains, 2:30
Sierra Nevada Mountains, 2:46
Sight, 3:136–137, 3:162–164, 5:17
Sight words, 5:34
Sikhs, 2:206
Silicon chip, 2:174
Silk, 2:151
Silt, 2:37, 2:53
Sinai Desert, 2:19
Sit-up, 3:213
Skeletal muscle, 3:137
Skeleton, 3:131–134
Skin, 3:122, 3:128–130, 3:220–221
Skull, 3:132
Sky, 2:60
    color, 2:54
    myths about, 2:61
Skylab, 2:91–92, 2:222
Slate, 2:53
Slavery, 2:39, 4:18–21, 4:162–163,
    4:166
Sleep, 3:217
Sloth, 3:76
Small intestine, 3:152, 3:154
Smallpox, 2:149–150, 3:177
Smell, 3:170–174, 5:18
Smith, Captain John, 4:105
Smoking, 3:193–195
Smooth muscle, 3:138
Snakes, 3:41, 3:75–76, 3:102–3

"Snow White and the Seven Dwarfs",
    1:22–30
Snowy owls, 3:60
Soccer, 2:267–271
Social studies, 5:56–58
Social work, 4:42–43, 4:93–96
Software, 5:70–72
Soil, 2:50–51
Solar eclipse, 2:71
Solar flare, 2:66
Solar system, 2:72
Solar wind, 2:66
Solid fuel rocket, 2:85, 2:87
Solomon, king, 2:203
Sound waves, 2:162–163, 3:165–166
South Africa, 2:210, 4:73–75
South America, 2:12, 2:13, 2:29,
    2:32–35
    area, 2:32, 2:194
    geography, 2:32–33
    history, 2:203, 2:205, 2:208, 2:213
    population, 2:215
    See also specific countries
South Carolina, 2:239–240, 2:246–247
South China Sea, 2:196
South Dakota, 2:246–247
Southern hemisphere, 2:65
Soviet Union, 2:17, 2:27, 2:211–213
    area, 2:197
    population, 2:215
    See also Russia
Soyuz, 2:222
Space, 2:188
    absence of gravity, 2:92–93
    exploration, 2:91–96, 2:222–223
    life on other worlds, 2:88–90
    travel in, 2:212, 2:214, 2:223,
        4:212–216
    See also Satellites; specific heavenly
        bodies
Spain, 2:30, 2:35, 2:205, 2:206, 2:212,
    4:149, 4:150
Spanish-American War, 2:214, 4:45,
    4:176–179